I0494260

Lean Accounting

By Ade Asefeso MCIPS MBA

Second Edition

ISBN-13: 978-1499397710
ISBN-10: 1499397712

Publisher: AA Global Sourcing Ltd
Website: http://www.aaglobalsourcing.com

Table of Contents

Disclaimer

This publication is designed to provide competent and reliable information regarding the subject matter covered. However, it is sold with the understanding that the author and publisher are not engaged in rendering professional advice. The authors and publishers specifically disclaim any liability that is incurred from the use or application of contents of this book.

Dedication

This book is dedicated to the hundreds of thousands of incredible souls in the world who have weathered through the up and down of recent recession.

To my family and friends who seems to have been sent here to teach me something about who I am supposed to be. They have nurtured me, challenged me, and even opposed me…. But at every juncture has taught me!

This book is dedicated to my lovely boys, Thomas, Michael and Karl. Teaching them to manage their finance will give them the lives they deserve. They have taught me more about life, presence, and energy management than anything I have done in my life.

Chapter 1: Introduction

You are aware of lean manufacturing, but did you know there is an accounting model that follows the same concept? Lean accounting is simply a different way of looking at the numbers.

Lean manufacturing and other lean operations initiatives create a company environment that demands a solution to the in-flexibility and low value of traditional cost accounting and financial reporting. Lean accounting, the proven alternative, enables the finance and accounting functions to partner with the evolving lean enterprise. When the finance department revamps their processes with lean methods, the time savings and communication gains are fantastic. Lean accounting provides a stage that enables the accounting team to move from a transaction focus to a new high value role of consulting within other areas of the company.

What is Lean Accounting?

It is the application of lean principles to the accounting and associated functions within the enterprise. The idea is simple, but the application is not obvious within the framework of traditional accounting systems.

What does it do?
- Identifies and eliminates non-value add waste in the accounting process and reporting processes.

- Improves visual reporting on product lines.
- Usually leads to the elimination of standard cost accounting.
- Adheres to all GAAP recommendations.
- Realigns accounting activities to a consulting role rather than a transaction role.

Lean accounting has two distinct areas that may be applied at different times on your lean journey.

"Lean for Accounting" = Applying lean tools (5S, process or value stream mapping, kaizens, etc.) to streamline the processes within the accounting and finance functions to minimize the consumption of resources and eliminating waste.

"Accounting for Lean" = Modifying traditional financial statements and reports to provide "Plain English Financial Statements" throughout the enterprise.

While there is a distinct differentiation between these two areas, the broader term "lean accounting" is often applied to both interchangeably.

Chapter 2: The History of Lean Accounting

The purpose of this chapter is to describe Lean Accounting in its current form, as it has evolved and sharpened in the years ensuing from that first meeting of the Lean Accounting Thought Leaders.

The most noteworthy evolution of Lean Accounting in recent years is a sharpening focus on value. While lean has always been centred on creating value for customers, and eliminating non-value adding waste, the companies deploying Lean Accounting and the researchers furthering our understanding of it are increasingly moving 'Value Adding' and Non-Value Adding' from the theoretical realm to a very specific, measurable one.

From isolating non-value adding expenses on Profit and Loss statements to using Value Adding Ratios, Lean Accounting is increasingly enabling manufacturers to specifically measure value in financial terms and to focus improvement efforts on enhancing value.

Origins and Evolution of Lean Accounting

September, 2012 marks the seventh anniversary of a momentous gathering in Dearborn, Michigan of a handful of the leading lean manufacturing practitioners, consultants and academics to formalize and unify the work they had been doing independently on a radically different approach to accounting for manufacturing which has become known as Lean Accounting. Since that time the annual Lean Accounting Summit has grown to include hundreds of participants and companies, and there are now thousands of manufacturing organizations around the world practicing Lean Accounting to varying degrees.

The expansion of Lean Accounting from that original small group has driven an evolution of the principles and practices as more companies are contributing to the body of knowledge based on practical experience, and a growing number of academic and manufacturing experts are studying and contributing to the enhancement of the underlying principles.

Lean Accounting evolved from a concern that traditional accounting practices were inadequate and, in fact, a deterrent to the adoption of some of the necessary improvements to manufacturing operations. While manufacturing managers knew that investments in automation and the adoption of lean manufacturing practices were the right things to do, traditional accounting was often an obstacle to such improvements, yielding numbers that only supported investments when they could be justified by reductions in direct labour, with little benefit ascribed to any improvements to quality, flexibility or factory throughput. Adoption of lean manufacturing practices was treated even worse, as reductions in factory cycle times drove corresponding reductions in inventories, triggering an under-absorption of overhead expenses and actually making the company appear to be less profitable as a result of their lean strategy.

The problems presented by traditional accounting reached an especially critical point in the 1980's as foreign largely Japanese competition took a severe toll on American manufacturing competitiveness. "Relevance Lost – The Rise and Fall of Management Accounting" written by Tom Johnson and Bob Kaplan in 1991 gave the problems with traditional accounting a very high level of visibility. A consortium effort coordinated by Computer Aided Manufacturing – International (CAM-I) brought the leading manufacturers and the academic community together over the course of a few years in the late 1980's to develop solutions, and the concept of Activity Based Cost Management resulted from their efforts. At about the same time, Eliyahu Goldratt's Theory of Constraints included the concept of Throughput Accounting, as another solution to the problem.

Activity Based Costing turned out to not be the hoped for solution, largely because it is primarily a more sophisticated approach to allocating costs and allocations are at the heart of the problem with traditional accounting. The solution is to eliminate allocations, rather than improve them. Goldratt's Throughput Accounting was much closer to the solution, although it did not provide sufficient structure and information to drive the elimination of non-value adding expenses, or 'waste' in lean terms.

11

Cornerstone of Lean Management

One of the most significant evolutions in the field of Lean Accounting is a growing awareness that Lean Accounting is actually the cornerstone of a completely different model of manufacturing management; an entirely different business model. By itself, Lean Accounting has limited value, but as the financial basis for the architecture and application of logistics, quality management, factory operations, marketing and pricing, and other critical business functions, Lean Accounting is extraordinarily powerful.

A core principle of Lean Accounting is that the Value Stream is the only appropriate cost collection entity within the organization, as opposed to traditional accounting's use of cells, cost or profit centres or departments normally based on smaller, functional groupings of work activity. The value stream is the complete sequence of activities within the organization that operationally links the incoming supply chain with one or more outgoing distribution channels, as well as the complete sequence of associated business activities required to take a customer order from start to finish. Only by assessing financial impact in the Value Stream structure can management be assured that a dollar saved at some point in the process did not trigger two dollars to be spent elsewhere.

The former Toyota Manufacturing Director Taichi Ohno once described their system saying, "All we are doing is looking at the time line from the moment the customer gives us an order to the point when we collect the cash. And we are reducing the time line by removing the non-value added wastes." This accurately describes the driving principle of lean manufacturing, and the model Lean Accounting supports. That "time line" from order to cash is the value stream. As manufacturers deploy lean practices and implement Lean Accounting it becomes increasingly apparent that restructuring the organization formally around value streams, rather than traditional functional, hierarchical lines, makes sense. Further, as the manufacturer increasingly focuses on reducing cycle times through the value stream and using Lean Accounting information to identify and eliminate waste, a number of other alternatives to traditional management theories become more effective. The driving principle at Motorola behind the origination of Six Sigma was "The best quality producer is the shortest cycle time producer, and the shortest cycle time producer is always the best cost producer." Goldratt's Theory of Constraints was similarly focused on the rate of flow through the business from start to finish as the critical driver of results. As all the state of the art in manufacturing management thinking aligns with Ohno's principle of process cycle times of processes and processes are synonymous with value streams an entire flow and waste elimination management scheme has emerged. In recent years it has become apparent that Lean Accounting cannot be discussed without discussing the broader lean management infrastructure it entails and supports.

While there is minor disagreement among Lean Accounting proponents and practitioners whether a conversion to Lean Accounting should best lead or follow the deployment of lean manufacturing practices on the shop floor and a transition to a lean manufacturing management model, there is no disagreement that Lean Accounting supports and is tightly integrated with a comprehensive Lean Enterprise, and that it does not stand alone as an accounting approach within the context of a traditional management scheme, or a factory pursuing old batch production theory of manufacturing

Core Principles

Lean Accounting is based on a number of core principles that represent a departure from traditional manufacturing management accounting principles.

Management First: Lean Accounting is based on the idea that accurate information for management analysis and decision making comes first, and that financial statements in accordance with GAAP can be derived from the Lean Accounting data. Traditional management and cost accounting is the reverse of this principle, starting with GAAP compliant accounting statements, and then attempting to derive information for management from those statements. Effective management information cannot be derived from traditionally developed external reports.

Value Centred: The most fundamental purpose of management accounting is to clearly differentiate between expenses for activities that add value and expense for activities that do not add value. All financial information presented to management should make this differentiation between value adding and waste clear.

Holistic Approach: Products and customers cannot be profitable or unprofitable. All sales (unless a product is being sold at a price below its direct material costs) contribute to the potential profitability of the business to varying degrees. Traditional cost accounting methods that attempt to determine product or customer profitability do so by means of allocations of expenses that are not directly related to the product or the sale, and introduce harmful distortions and lead to erroneous management conclusions. Decisions regarding pricing make versus buy and capital investments must be made holistically, based on the overall impact the decision will have on the contribution level of the value stream.

Value Stream Structured: The Value Stream is the appropriate entity within the organization for gathering, summarizing and analyzing expenses for purposes of management control and decision making. A Value Stream includes all of the cross-functional physical and human resources required to process a customer order from creation to collection, linking externally at both ends from the customer and the supply chain to the customer and the distribution channels. The objective of each value stream is to focus resources and improvement efforts on the creation of value for customers, and the elimination of activities and expenses that do not contribute to adding customer value. Because different customers, or different categories of customers, define value in different manners, a Value Stream should be created for each significant customer defined value requirement.

For example a company manufacturing and selling machined components to both the automotive market and the aerospace market would create a value stream for each of those markets since the requirements of automotive and aerospace will be quite different in a number of ways. This differentiation should occur even if the products sold to each market are quite similar. The objective is not cost reduction through economy of scale, but enhancement of overall value, which is much broader than simple direct unit cost reduction.

Cash Based – Plain English: Lean Accounting treats virtually all costs other than direct material as period costs. One critical objective of Lean Accounting is to simplify the financial statements and put them in a format that is easily understood by everyone in the organization in order to more fully engage the organization at all levels in the effort to reduce non-value adding expenses. Full absorption and moving expenses to the balance sheet per the Matching Principle are the primary culprits in creating misleading and harmful accounting information for manufacturing. By minimizing or eliminating allocations of indirect costs to production, and valuing inventories at as close as possible to direct material costs, this effect is eliminated, or minimized. Lean Accounting strives to enable management to understand and interpret the financial information in a manner that closely approximates how people account for their own lives at home, with a heavy reliance on cash flows and the ability to assess spending as it actually occurs.

Fixed Costs: Lean Accounting is biased toward an assumption that all costs are fixed, rather than variable. Because all costs are generally fixed in the very short term, and generally variable in the long term, assigning a cost to either fixed or variable status depends entirely on the time frame for which the cost is being assessed. Further, most 'costs' are not single costs at all, rather they are collections of like costs. Machine maintenance, for instance, is apt to include both labour and maintenance supplies, and both planned and unplanned activities. It has multiple elements each with multiple drivers. Some aspects of the expense may tend to be fixed; maintenance labour for instance, while other elements may be more variable breakdown parts and supplies, for example.

Since all costs are both fixed and variable and the true behaviours are likely to be unknowable, the determining factor is management control. If costs are classified as variable (as traditional accounting assumes them to be in allocating them to each unit of production), management has much looser control and visibility than if they were assumed to be fixed. If they are assumed to be variable, then management has essentially given the organization license to increase spending in those cost areas proportionate to sales volumes. A 5% increase in sales, for instance, allows operations to increase spending by 5% even though a significant element of the expense should

17

not vary with volume. On the other hand, when management assumes costs to be fixed, increases in volume do not trigger an allowance to increase spending proportionately, and any increase will generate a spending variance, enhancing management's ability to delve into and understand cost increases. In summary, an assumption of fixed behaviour increases managerial cost control in a growing organization to a much greater degree than assuming costs are variable.

Perhaps most important, a cornerstone of lean is respect for the necessity of involving everyone in the ongoing control and improvement of processes. This cannot be accomplished without providing basic job security. Lean companies cannot succeed by laying off and recalling employees as short term sales volumes may require. Labour, therefore, is a fixed cost and leveraging that cost by steadily increasing volumes is critical to profitability.

Chapter 3: Lean Accounting and Traditional Accounting

If you are already a Lean Accounting enthusiast, this chapter will be a handy review for you. You already understand the value and importance of what you are doing. If you are not familiar with Lean Accounting, then I hope this chapter and the next few chapters will help you understand enough to make an informed judgment for your company.

So here we go.

Costing

I am going to start with some definitions.

Standard Costing is an accounting technique in which standard product costs are calculated for every part, sub-assembly, and finished product. Throughout the operations that use or produce the part, detailed "actual" information is gathered. After all the costs are in (usually after month-end) these are compared with the "actual" costs, and reports are created to analyze the variances from standard.

Typically, a standard costing system is complex to set up and requires millions of wasteful and time-consuming entries of the "actual" data. I am using the word "waste" in the Lean context as "any activity that does not add value in the eyes of the customer." Very few people in the company understand how the standard costs are calculated and yet they are expected to improve them, make decisions based on them, and even price products using them.

Value Stream Costing is an accounting method using actual cost information to record the revenues, spending, cash flow, and profits of the company's value streams as a whole. Value Stream Costing usually does not need to address the costs of individual products, although there are methods to do this if required. When a company is making good progress with Lean Thinking and methods, all the reporting, analysis, and decision-making can be done better at the value stream level.

Lean organizations manage their business by the value streams. The value streams are where the value is created and the money is made. Value Stream Costing is entirely aligned with the value stream. It is quick, simple and timely. It is clear and easy for non-financial people to understand and to act upon because it directly addresses the value stream structure. It requires very few transactions because the information is collected at a higher level. It also supports Lean performance measurements and the Lean Box Score.

Why is this important?

If a company is working to become a Lean enterprise and continues to use standard costing methods (or it's bigger and more complicated brothers like activity-based costing, RCA, and others) the financial reporting will motivate anti-Lean behaviours among the people working in the company. The variance reports will lead them to sub-optimize the value stream flow and costs. The overhead absorption variances will motivate large batches, over-production, long lead times, and high inventories.

The decisions made using traditional standard costing will in a Lean environment lead to bad decisions. In the competitive global business environment where we find ourselves today, it is impossible to overstate the importance of this. That is why I am devoting an entire chapter of this subject. For now, let's just say the company will turn away good work based on standard cost "profit margins."

Lean companies are constantly striving for simplicity and transparency. The complexity of standard costing creates waste. The opacity of standard costing leads to bad decisions. The huge number of wasteful transactions required to support standard costing (and the reports, meetings, and reconciliations) drains the people's time and degrades productivity.

As you can see, the difference between Lean Accounting and Traditional Accounting impacts all five of the Lean Principles, namely:
1. Customer Value
2. Value Streams
3. Flow and Pull
4. Empowered People
5. The Pursuit of Perfection.

I will leave you with these thoughts; Traditional Standard Costing focuses on hundreds or thousands of cost centres. Lean Accounting focuses on the company's (relatively few) value streams because this is where the value is created. This is where the customers' needs are understood and fully met. This is where the company turns value into profit and cash flow.

Chapter 4: Main Thrusts of Lean Accounting

There are two main thrusts for Lean Accounting. The first is the application of lean methods to the company's accounting, control, and measurement processes. This is no different than applying lean methods to any other processes. The objective is to eliminate waste, free up capacity, speed up the process, eliminate errors and defects, and make the process clear and understandable.

The second (and more important) thrust of Lean Accounting is to fundamentally change the accounting, control, and measurement processes so they motivate lean change and improvement, provide information that is suitable for control and decision-making, provide an understanding of customer value, correctly assess the financial impact of lean improvement, and are themselves simple, visual, and low-waste.

Lean Accounting does not require the traditional management accounting methods like standard costing, activity-based costing, variance reporting, cost-plus pricing, complex transactional control systems, and untimely and confusing financial reports. These are replaced by lean-focused performance measurements simple summary direct costing of the value streams decision-making and reporting using a box score financial reports that are timely and presented in "plain language" that everyone can understand radical simplification and elimination of transactional control systems by eliminating the need for them driving lean changes from a deep understanding of the value created for the customers eliminating traditional budgeting through monthly sales, operations, and financial planning processes (SOFP) value-based pricing correct understanding of the financial impact of lean change.

As an organization becomes more mature with lean thinking and methods, they recognize that the combined methods of Lean Accounting in fact creates a Lean Management System (LMS) designed to provide the planning, the operational and financial reporting, and the motivation for change required to prosper the company's on-going lean transformation.

Up until 2006, the methods of Lean Accounting were not clearly defined because they had been developed by different people in different companies. A meeting was held at the 2005 Lean Accounting Summit (Lean Accounting Summit) conference including a number of leaders in the field, and a decision was made to develop a document called "The Principles, Practices, and Tools of Lean Accounting" (PPT) (Lean Accounting PPT).

While the methods of lean accounting are continually evolving, the PPT lays out the primary methods of Lean Accounting and shows how they fit together into a Lean Management System. The PPT emphasizes not only the tools and methods of Lean Accounting, but also the need for focusing on customer value and the empowerment (or respect) for people.

Chapter 5: Lean Accounting Vision

The vision for Lean Accounting is to provide accurate, timely, and understandable information to motivate the lean transformation throughout the organization, and for decision-making leading to increased customer value, growth, profitability, and cash flow.

You can use lean tools to eliminate waste from the accounting processes while maintaining thorough financial control and fully comply with generally accepted accounting principles (GAAP), external reporting regulations, and internal reporting requirements.

You can support the lean culture by motivating investment in people, providing information that is relevant and actionable, and empowering continuous improvement at every level of the organization.

Why is lean accounting needed?

There are positive and negative reasons for using Lean Accounting. The positive reasons include the issues addressed in the "Vision for Lean Accounting" shown above. Lean Accounting provides accurate, timely and understandable information that can be used by managers, sales people, operations leaders, accountants, lean improvement teams and others. The information gives clear insight into the company's performance; both operational and financial. The

Lean Accounting reporting motivates people in the organization to move lean improvement forward. It is often stated that "what you measure is what will be improved." Lean accounting measures the right things for a company that wants to drive forward with lean transformation.

Lean Accounting is also itself lean. The information, reports, and measurements can be provided quickly and easily. It does not require the complex systems and wasteful transactions that are usually used by manufacturing companies.

The simplicity of Lean Accounting frees up the time of the financial people and the operational people so that they can become more actively involved in moving the company forward towards its strategic goals. The role of the financial professional moves away from bookkeeper and reporter and towards strategic partnering with the company leaders.

At a deeper level Lean Accounting matches the cultural goals of a lean organization. The simple and timely information empowers people at all levels of the organization. The financial and performance measurement information is organized around value streams and thereby honours the lean principle of value stream management.

The emphasis on customer value is also derived from the principles of lean thinking. The way a company accounts and measures its business is deeply rooted in the culture of the organization. Lean Accounting has an important role to play in developing a lean culture within an organization.

Why is traditional accounting not needed?

The negative reasons for using Lean Accounting lie with the inadequacy of traditional accounting systems to support a lean culture. Everybody working seriously on the lean transformation of their company eventually bumps up against their accounting systems. Traditional accounting systems (particularly those using standard costing, activity-based costing, or other full absorption methods) are designed to support traditional management methods. As a company moves to lean thinking, many of the fundamentals of its management system change and traditional accounting, control, and measurement methods become unsuitable. Some examples of this are:

1. Traditional accounting systems are large, complex processes requiring a great deal of non-value work. Lean companies are anxious to eliminate this kind of non-value work.

2. They provide measurements and reports like labour efficiency and overhead absorption that motivate large batch production and high inventory levels. These measurements are suitable for mass production-style organizations but actively harmful to companies with lean aspirations.

3. The traditional accounting systems have no good way to identify the financial impact of the lean improvements taking place

29

throughout the company. On the contrary, the financial reports will often show that bad things are happening when very good lean change is being made. One example of this is that traditional reporting shows a reduction in profitability when inventory is reduced. Lean companies always make significant inventory reductions and the accounting reports show negative results.

4. Traditional accounting reports use technical words and methods like "overhead absorption", "gross margin", and many others. These reports are not widely understood within most organizations. This may be acceptable when the financial reports are restricted to senior managers, but a lean company will seek to empower the entire workforce. Clear and understandable reporting is required so that people can readily use the reports for improvement and decision-making.

5. Traditional companies use standard product (or service) costs which can be misleading when making decisions related to quoting, profitability, make/buy, sourcing, product rationalization, and so forth. Lean companies seek to have a clearer understanding of the true costs associated with their processes and value streams.

There are of course traditional methods for overcoming some of these issues and problems.

Indeed, few of the methods of Lean Accounting are new ideas. They are mostly adaptations of methods that have been used for many years, and have been codified into a Lean Management System designed to support the needs of lean thinking organizations.

Where does Lean Accounting apply?

As with most lean methods Lean Accounting was developed to support manufacturing companies, and most of the implementation of Lean Accounting has been within manufacturing organizations. Now that lean methods are moving into other industries like financial services, healthcare, government, and education there are some initial examples of the application of Lean Accounting in these industries.

Chapter 6: Applying Lean to Accounting

Customer focus is a critical element in lean thinking. Do you set the pace of production to the customer demand rate (the Takt time)? Is the Voice of the Customer (VOC) used in product and service design? The answer is always an emphatic "Yes". The customer is always critical to improvement activities.

But, as lean product/service companies start to address the vast lean waste reduction potential in back office areas such as Accounting, they are finding that for many employees, the concept of the "customer" can be confusing, difficult, and just maybe hasn't been considered before. Who is their customer? Even asking the question can bring confusion, strange looks, and, often, silence.

The first answer for many is the boss or management. When asked to reconsider, the next response is usually a department, then another department, then the employees, then the executive team, then the stockholders, and before you know it, everyone is "the customer". Unfortunately, none of these guesses are helpful with improvement activities. And, there is not an accurate, concise definition that fits every company.

The first step in solving this mystery is to distinguish between the external customer (the entity that buys the product or service of the organization) and the internal customer (the person or part of the organization that will receive the benefit of the process being performed). It should always be noted that the internal customer need never trumps the external customer need.

Next, think about what work or activities directly affects the external customer. In Accounting, it will include collection activities at a minimum and maybe contract administration and certain investor relations activities. These types of activities are high priority opportunities for waste elimination through quality improvement, VOC input, and pace setting information.

However, to really engage and improve the functions that support the company in meeting the external customers' overall needs, it is essential to identify who is the internal customer for every action that is done in these support processes. One way to visualize this is to think of the flow of water. It starts upstream and flows down; always moving toward a destination. So, in Accounting "streams", what is upstream (the "suppliers") of the work being done? What is downstream (the internal customers)? The downstream is usually the best indicator of the internal customer, but not always. Be sure to dig deep downstream for a true identification.

A second way to identify the customer of a process is to ask, "Why do we do this process?" Ask the "why" question several times with no preconceived notion of the answer. Once you have a very simple answer of why the work is done, an activity statement can be written and used as a proxy for the customer in that process.

Chapter 7: Application of Lean to Accounting Processes

In the early stages of lean it is important to apply lean improvement throughout the organization; and there is nowhere more suitable than the accounting processes. These include the month-end close, accounts payable, accounts receivable, payroll, cost accounting, expense reporting, and so forth.

There are three reasons for applying lean improvement methods to the accounting processes:
1. The processes will be improved and the company's operations made better.
2. The finance people will learn a lot about lean methods.
3. Lean is not learned from books but by actual hands-on experience.

The removal of waste will free up time for the finance people to work on the introduction of Lean Accounting.

Some people object to making changes to the accounting processes because they ask why we would want to spend time making processes better when in fact we will be eliminating them in the future. The answer to this is that with lean we are always interested in making many small improvements. We are not looking for the "silver bullet" that will solve all problems. On the contrary, we are looking to engage the entire work force in many smaller changes that lead to massive improvement over time. It is, of course, our objective over time to largely eliminate most of these wasteful accounting processes, but at the earlier stages of lean change we are content to improve the processes, provide learning to the finance people, and free up their time for the more significant lean changes in the future.

Lean performance measurements

The control of the production (and other) processes is achieved by visual performance measurements at the shop-floor and value stream level. These measurements eliminate the need for the shop-floor tracking and variance reporting favoured by traditional cost accounting systems. There are (at least) three levels of operational performance measurements.

	Purpose	Plan Do Check Act Improve	Typical Frequency
Company or Plant Measurements	Enable the senior managers of the company monitor the achievement of the company's strategy.	Strategy Deployment	Monthly
Value Stream Measurements	Track the performance of the value stream and provide information to drive continuous improvement (CI).	Continuous Improvement	Weekly
Cell and Process Measurements	Enable the cell team to monitor and control their own activities.	Identify defects and eliminate them	Hourly or by shift

Continuous improvement (CI) is motivated and tracked using value stream performance boards. Typically these visual boards are updated weekly and used by the value stream CI team to identify improvement areas, initiate projects, and monitor their progress. These boards show the value stream performance measurements, Pareto charts (or other root cause analysis), and information about the CI projects. The boards also show the current and future state maps together with the project plan to move from current to future state. The Value Stream Performance Boards become "mission control" for both break-through improvement and continuous improvement of the value stream.

Typical measurements include:
- Productivity (sales/person).
- Process control (on-time shipment to customer requirement).
- Flow (dock-to-dock days or hours).
- Quality and Standardized Work (first time through without scrap or rework).
- Linearity and overall improvement (average cost).
- People participating in Continuous Improvement.
- Safety (Safety cross showing lost time, accidents, near-misses, etc.)

Cell and process measurements are reported frequently of 10 hourly by the people working in the cell or the process. The measurements are used to control the process and identify defects. When defects are identified they are "fixed" in the short term to serve the customers today and solved over the longer term so that they never occur again.

Typical measurements include:
- Day-by-the-Hour production quantities.
- First Time Thru without scrap or rework.
- WIP to SWIP (work-in-process inventory within the cell or process compared to the

standard work-in-process required within the process).

- Operational equipment effectiveness – OEE (for machine driven operations and particularly for bottleneck or constraint machines.)

Financial Reports for Lean Operations

Costs Included in Value Stream Costing*

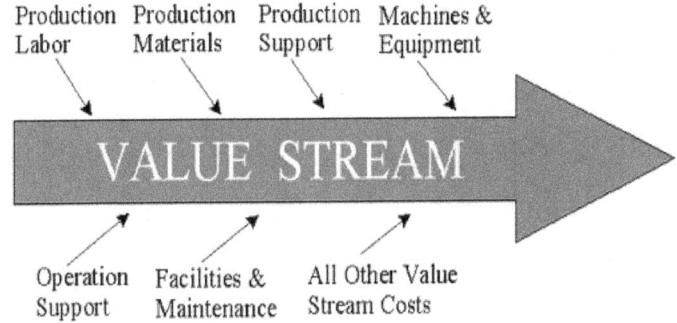

Cost and profitability reporting is achieved using Value Stream Costing, a simple summary direct costing of the value streams. The value stream costs are typically collected weekly and there is little or no allocation of "overheads." This provides financial information that can be clearly understood by everybody in the value stream which in turn leads to good decisions, motivation to lean improvement across the entire value stream, and clear accountability

41

for cost and profitability. Weekly reporting also provides excellent control and management of costs because they can be reviewed by the value stream manager while the information is still current.

Plain language financial statements

Lean accounting provides financial reports that are readily understandable to anyone in the company. The income statements are in "plain language" and the information is presented in a way that is no more complicated than a household budget. Plain language income statements are easy to use because they do not include misleading and confusing data relating to standard costs and hosts of incomprehensible variance figures. When used in meetings, plain language financial statements change the question from "What does this mean?" to "What should we do?"

Box Score reporting

Box Scores are used widely within lean accounting. The standard format of the box score shows a 3-dimensional view of value stream performance; operational performance measurements, financial performance, and how the value stream capacity is being used. The capacity information shows how much of the capacity within the value stream is used productively, how much is used to do non-productive activities, and how much value stream capacity is available for use. The box score shows the value stream performance on a single sheet of paper and using a simple and accessible format.

Box scores are used for decision-making, for assessing the financial impact of lean improvement, for selecting or prioritizing such issues as capital acquisitions using the 3P approach, and other reporting and decision-making requirements. Companies using lean accounting often have a standard box score format and require that all decisions relating to a value stream be presented using the standard box scores. This leads to operational and financial information being consistent and well understood when it is used.

Product or service costing

Under most circumstances it is not necessary to calculate product or service costs. Traditional manufacturing companies usually calculate a fully absorbed product cost using complex methods for the allocation of overhead costs, and they use these product costs for decision-making, inventory valuation, and performance measurements in the form of variance analysis and such metrics as individual efficiency. Similar methods are used in service organizations to estimate the cost of each service they provide.

Companies employing lean accounting methods recognize that standard costs and other methods for fully absorbed product or service costing lead to poor decisions and motivate anti-lean behaviour. These companies also find that there is no need to calculate a product cost because all the uses of product costs within traditional companies can be addressed in lean accounting using simpler and better methods.

43

Decision-making, inventory valuation, performance measurements, and other uses of fully absorbed product costs are all achieved using other lean accounting methods. If a product cost is required for reporting international transfer pricing, for example; then these can be calculated using simpler and more lean-focused methods like Features and Characteristics costing.

External Reporting closing the books

The primary collection of revenue and costs is done using Value Stream Costing, and (typically) weekly value stream income statements are used by the value stream managers to control costs and work to reduce costs. A typical lean organization will have several revenue earning or order fulfilment value streams, one or two new product development value streams, and then a small group of people and departments that support the value streams but are not in the value streams. These external support people include, for example, a plant or division manager, HR, Information systems, and so forth. The costs of these support people are relatively small in comparison to the value streams.

External reporting is achieved by taking the monthly value stream income statements and the financial statement for the support people and adding them together to provide the consolidated financial report for the company or division as a whole. This month-end close provides financial reports for the company that can be used for all external reporting. There is usually a requirement for some "below the line"

44

adjustments to bring the income state in line with generally accepted accounting principles (GAAP). These adjustments include any change of inventory value between now and last month, group and corporate overhead allocations, and other miscellaneous adjustments like exchange rate gains and losses. The "bottom line" of the adjusted statement will of course be the same as the traditional statements. There is no formal change of accounting method and the bottom line will therefore be the same.

Lean Accounting Closing the Books Example.

	Cartridge	Manifold	Flexible	Temperature	New Products	Support	Total
	April-10	April-10	April-10	April-10	April-10	April-10	April-10
Sales	$3,412,726	$719,315	$3,494,895	$969,215			$8,596,150
Commissions	$153,178	$32,286	$156,866	$43,503			$385,833
Wages & Fringes	$1,179,256	$313,930	$784,958	$152,914	$402,354	$215,339	$3,048,751
Materials	$836,141	$148,519	$793,457	$453,886	$12,778	$18,005	$2,262,786
Freight	$54,619	$3,779	$78,034	$3,446	$12,043	$3,214	$155,135
Supplies & Tooling	$68,438	$24,950	$31,936	$13,068	$51,833	$1,256	$191,481
Outside Services	$118,903	$2,000	$114,212	$0	$2,109	$4,600	$241,824
Depreciation	$12,876	$6,962	$33,052	$15,959	$32,577	$2,399	$103,825
Rentals	$10,637	$0	$0	$0			$10,637
Facilities / Utilities	$18,763	$6,031	$20,773	$5,361	$5,696	$10,387	$67,011
T&E	$2,146	$768	$3,411	$488	$1,982	$4,366	$13,161
Warranty	$51,191	$10,790	$52,423	$14,538			$128,942
Other	$8,630	$6,465	$18,261	$3,405		$20,149	$56,910
TOTAL COSTS	$2,514,778	$556,480	$2,087,384	$706,568	$521,372	$279,715	$6,666,296
VALUE STREAM PROFIT	$897,948	$162,835	$1,407,511	$262,647	($521,372)	($279,715)	$1,929,854
Value Stream Margin %	26%	23%	40%	28%	-6%	-3%	22%

Inventory change adjustment	$54,933
Exchange rate adjustment	($3,266)
Corporate overheads	($300,865)
NET PROFIT	**$1,680,656**

Inventory valuation

An important aspect of financial control is the evaluation of inventory. Lean manufacturing always leads to substantial inventory reductions. When inventories are low and under good control (using pull systems, single-piece flow, supplier partnerships, etc.), the valuation of inventory becomes much less complex. Lean Accounting contains a number of methods for valuing inventory that are simple, accurate, and often visual. Several of these methods do not require any computer-based inventory tracking at all.

Compliance to regulatory requirements

A question that always comes up when discussing lean accounting is whether these methods comply with regulatory accounting requirements and GAAP (generally accepted accounting principles). Lean accounting fully complies with all statutory and generally accepted accounting requirements in the United States and Europe, including the unique requirements of German, Swiss, and Italian regulation. Lean accounting also complies with the increasingly popular International Accounting Standards (IAS) that is seeking to create a single world-wide approach. When moving from traditional accounting methods to lean accounting there is no "change of accounting" because the external reporting outcome of lean accounting uses the same accrual based actual costing required by GAAP and statutory regulations. There is an argument that lean accounting lends itself better to statutory regulations because they require reporting at actual cost. Lean accounting uses actual costs throughout, whereas traditional accounting uses standard costs that must then be adjusted to actual costing for external reporting.

Chapter 8: Lean Accounting Value Stream Profit and Loss

The value stream structure enables management to see resources and their associated costs aligned with the various channels or market segments the company serves, a critical insight that is usually impossible to distinguish in companies with traditional organization structures and traditional accounting statements.

The sorting by expenses into value adding and non-value adding, then further breaking the non-value adding expenses down into operational waste of the sort which is the focus of lean manufacturing tools; management controlled expenses which do not add value to the customer but may add value to the business or represent investments in improving the value adding capability in the future; and required expenses which include items that do not add value to the customer but are necessary to comply with laws and regulations, is an important breakdown in Lean Accounting statements in that it provides management with a clear picture of the organizations ability to add value, and where waste can be found that may be a target for elimination.

Elimination of Waste

The goal of the lean manufacturer is not cost reduction so much as it is the elimination of expenses that do not add value in the eyes of the customer. The lean manufacturer does not necessarily seek to be the lowest cost producer so much as to be the best value producer.

A few brave finance and accounting managers are changing how they track costs to support lean manufacturing and improve decision making.

As wary as executives are these days of anything that smacks of "creative" accounting, there is a quiet revolution unfolding among lean manufacturers. The idea creeping into the heads of a few radical thinkers is that the financial numbers reported should actually reflect the underlying reality of the business. Armed with more relevant information, business unit managers could then make better decisions when it came to product pricing, make-versus-buy questions, and product and customer rationalization.

Falling under the general heading of "lean accounting," the approach does not require any new math or tricky algorithms. But it does demand a fundamental change in perspective. A unit of our company had an opportunity to bid on a component with a market price of £3.75. The standard accounting showed it would cost £4.61 for the unit to make and sell the product.

We took a look at it and recognized that from a traditional cost accounting standpoint, this would be a loser, when in fact, if you go through lean processes and look at out-of-pocket expenses, we actually come away with a very profitable application.

Material accounted for £1 with standard cost calculations, and the remainder was for labour and overhead. But because the company had the capacity to make the product on existing equipment, and because the additional labour required to run the machine was negligible, the new product would essentially cost us only the price of the raw material. And the difference between the price and material cost would drop to the bottom line. We did successfully bid for the order, and reaped a six-figure contribution to quarterly profits.

Standard cost tells you that for every dollar/pounds of material you bring on, you are going to have an incremental amount of labour and spending, and that is just not true,". Essentially, the lean-accounting approach treats many of the costs typically regarded as variable as fixed, depending upon available capacity and the real investments in people and equipment required.

The lean accounting movement was born of frustration. Many manufacturers that have used the techniques championed by Toyota to reduce set-up times and convert from batch production methods to work-cells and one-piece flow don't immediately realize the results on the bottom line. In fact, during the transition, which can stretch over a number of years, net earnings take a hit as obsolete inventory is written down. If sales remain flat, lower production volumes caused by the reduction of excess inventory also increase the overhead burden on the remaining output.

Lean accounting proponents argue that lean production operations simply cannot be measured in the same way that traditional batch manufacturing is. Traditional accounting methods encourage high-volume production runs that fully absorb overhead and build work-in-process and finished-goods inventory. They reflect the era in which they were developed, which was characterized by less product variety and economy-of-scale thinking. What is more, using the information generated by traditional methods can lead to decisions that are not only wrongheaded, but tragic.

A manager at an FTSE 250 company tells the story of a factory in one its division hit by a market downturn and subsequent lower sales volumes. This reduced overhead absorption, which increased the overhead and led to an increase in prices that reduced sales even further. Hastening this death spiral, rather than source products from this plant, which had plenty of available capacity, other business units within the division purchased parts from outside suppliers because of non-competitive transfer prices based upon standard cost plus 15%.

If the products had been priced to accurately reflect the incremental cost of production, the internal customers would have paid less in-house than they did outside. Eventually, company executives chose to shut down the under-utilized plant.

At heart, the lean accounting approach takes a simpler look at what goes on between the inputs and outputs of a production process, tracking costs in less-minute detail, expensing material as soon as it is pulled into production, and eliminating work orders, the tracking of transactions and the reporting of variances altogether. Many manufacturing plants today rely on such activities to monitor product costs and track the value of inventory. But, lean-accounting advocates say that such procedures are inherently wasteful.

Before a manufacturer can drop such activities, however, the production operation has to be far enough into lean manufacturing to be organized by value streams, a customer-centric structure that pulls together all of the fulfilment functions from order receipt to delivery. Under a lean accounting system each value stream has its own, slightly modified, profit-and-loss statement. Traditional financial statements are still needed to satisfy auditors and reporting requirements, but these statements aren't used to run the business. The ultimate result; Accountants give up their roles as traffic cops and start providing the type of analysis and reports that make decision-making more straightforward, rather than a battle over the accuracy of the numbers.

From a financial perspective, when you create a true value stream cells with all of the work centres connected to each other the investment decision when you are looking at equipment is so much easier to make. I am sitting here in my office right now, and I have a value stream map hanging on the wall, I know I can improve certain operations in those data boxes I have up there, but it will do me no good in getting product through the system to the customer, unless I improve this particular operation first. Such constraints are invisible in a standard printout from accounting that lists how many minutes or hours are required at each operation.

I know it is hard for managers to give up methods taught in business school and abandon the metrics that they have always used to track performance. Lean accounting also has a broad impact on the organization. In addition to adoption by the accounting and finance departments, it requires buy-in from managers in engineering, purchasing, IT and customer service. Getting all of these people on board is difficult, if not impossible, without a mandate from the top.

Those who have begun to change the way they track financials say it is worth the effort. If asked directly, few CEOs and even controllers can explain what drives all of their variances or how they are calculated. But when the numbers make intuitive sense, and business performance isn't cloaked in accounting jargon, people at all levels can make better and more profitable decisions.

It allows the workforce to understand what they are spending i.e., what the input is to get a certain level of output. Then they can focus on how to do it better.

Still, making the transition requires some convincing. When looking at whether we can make an adequate profit at a certain market price, we often put a standard operating income statement next to a modified one to prove the point that a product that might not meet a gross margin test can actually be very beneficial to the bottom line.

People know and breathe and die by standard cost, they want to see it side-by-side and look at it incrementally and see where standard cost breaks down and where we can make a better decision.

Comparison of a traditional profit and loss statement (P&L) and a lean-accounting P&L. In the example below; high conversion costs reflect a capital-intensive business. The top and bottom line are the same in both examples. One advantage of the lean accounting P&L is that the types of costs are broken down into recognizable categories. If the company is trying to rein in procurement costs, for example, the impact of such efforts would be readily apparent on the P&L.

Plain English Profit and Loss Account

Traditional		
Sales	£9,570,000	100%
Cost of Sales	£6,364,758	66.5%
Gross Margin	£3,205,242	33.5%
Total Adjustments	£270,007	2.8%
Net Manufacturing Margin	£2,935,235	30.7%
Other Operating Costs	£738,164	7.7%
Net Operating Margin	£2,197,072	23%
Total Sales Expense	£139,358	1.5%
Net Operating Margin	£2,057,713	21.5%
Other Expense	£195,973	2%
Net Earning	£1,861,741	19.5%

Lean		
Sales	£9,570,000	100%
Costs		
Procurement	£910,184	9.5%
Conversion	£6,388,710	66.8%
Distribution	£337,509	3.5%
Support	£762,116	8%
Total Costs	£8,398,519	87.8%
Margin	£1,171,481	12.2%
Change in Inventory	£690,259	7.2%
Net earnings	£1,861,741	19.5%

Chapter 9: Lean Accounting Value Stream Management

Lean manufacturing has taken hold in increasingly greater numbers of United States and European manufacturing companies to improve throughput, efficiency, cycle-time and customer satisfaction. These improvements have put pressure on management systems geared to support the traditional method of manufacturing that use large batches and long production runs to achieve economies of scale. This chapter provides a framework for implementing systems and controls more suited to the lean company. It is divided into three dimensions of the lean management issue.

1. Developing an Appropriate Management Focus
2. Organizing by Value Stream
3. Costing by Value Stream

Developing an Appropriate Management Focus

Lean companies focus on creating value for customers. Value is created in the order fulfilment processes, from selling, to manufacturing, shipping and collection of cash, as well as after-sales support. Value is also created in the processes for identifying, developing and bringing to market new products and services. By locating the value creating processes next to one another and by processing one unit at a time, work flows smoothly from one step to another and finally to the customer. This chain of value-creating processes is called a value stream. A value stream is simply all the things done to create value for the customer. All products having similar features and characteristics are manufactured in one value stream. It could be said that a value stream is comprised of all products having the same routing through the company.

A typical value stream will fulfil customer orders through a process like this:

Typical Order Fulfilment Value Stream

Sales	Order Entry	Configure Product	Schedule	Purchase Materials

Invoicing	Ship Product to Customer	Manufacture Product	Materials Handling	Production Planning

| Collect Cash | | | Maintenance | |

| After Sales Support | | | Production Engineering | |

| | | | Cost Accounting | |

| | | | Quality Assurance | |

| | | | Customer Service | |

The value stream is far more than just the manufacturing processes. In the diagram above, manufacturing is shown as just one step in the whole process of serving the customer and creating value. There are many processes that support the manufacturing steps. Some companies make the mistake of defining their value streams too narrowly; they include only the production steps. It is important to see the value stream as including all the things required to create value for the customer.

Value streams can include more than just what occurs within the production plant. Organizations with finished goods warehouses usually include them in the value stream. The warehouse may be outside the immediate control of the plant people, but it contributes to both customer value and waste. Similarly, if the operation pulls materials from another plant within the same organization then this "supplier" will often be included as a part of the value stream. A company that sells through distributors may include the distributor as a part of its value streams in order to "see" the flow through to the end customer.

A lean organization needs to manage the flows of the work through the value streams. This entails a different management focus from the traditional company that is organized and managed by function. Prior to lean manufacturing, most companies were organized by production departments. These departments sometimes called centres of excellence; were designed to be highly efficient at performing one particular step in the process. A production step could be welding, stamping, surface mount insertion, assembly, burn-in, heat treat, and so forth. An organization of this kind cannot see the flow; it is too difficult to identify. As we move into value streams the flow becomes much clearer, and we can manage and improve the process.

The departmental organization, on the other hand, often becomes an obstacle to achieving a smooth flow of the product through the plant, as the focus becomes department efficiency rather than flow. Managing the flow of the work demands an understanding of the value streams and putting in place organizations and controls that are focused around them. The primary purpose of the manager in a lean company is to focus on value stream processes to work toward improving the flow of the work and the achievement of perfection in quality and customer satisfaction. That can only be achieved through a relentless focus on the place where value is created; the value steam.

We focus on value streams because this is the best way to see the flow of materials, information, and cash. It is the best way to understand and increase the value we are creating for the customer. And it is the best way to grow the business, increase sales, and generate more profit.

Organizing by Value Stream

As lean manufacturing matures within the company it becomes increasingly necessary to manage the value streams. Managers with Profit and Loss responsibility for the value stream need to be assigned. Growth and improvement strategies for the company now revolve around the value stream. A useful way to look at this is to imagine the company made up of several small, entrepreneurial companies; each one responsible for making their value streams a spectacular success. This form of organization is best for lean companies because it simplifies management of the lean company and because it provides the visibility for managing continuous improvement.

The Simplicity of the Value Stream Organization

The value stream focus greatly simplifies the management of the company.

Lean organizations are always striving for simplicity of operation. It is, of course, very difficult to make processes simple. You must eliminate the root causes of variability and bring the processes under control.

An example of simplicity at work is a kan-ban pull system. Kan-ban is very simple. When the card comes up you make some more. You make what the card tells you, and you make it immediately. But a production plant can only move from MRPII to kan-ban when the methods of lean manufacturing have been successful applied. You must have small batches, reliable processes, effective machines, and regular production cycle times. Moving from MRPII to kan-ban is a move from the over-complexity of traditional manufacturing to simplicity of operation.

Moving from a departmental organization to a value stream organization is a similar change. You move from a highly complex organization chart with hundreds of cost centres, thousands of transactions to keep track of people, and a bureaucracy to 3 or 4 value streams within the plant and a clear-cut line of responsibility.

This is simple not only because the people know where they should focus their work, but also it simplifies the performance reporting, the organization structure, the accounting reports, and other infrastructure processes. A well-run value stream has a team people working together to serve the customers, increase value, improve their performance measurements every week, and make a lot of money. It is simple, clear-cut, and effective.

Value Stream as the Locus for Improvement

Continuous improvement (CI) is achieved through the value streams. Lean organizations have CI teams assigned to each value stream. These are made up of people working in the value stream but may have some outsiders also. The purpose of the CI team is to review the value stream performance measurements each week and initiate projects to make these measurements improve every week.

There is a place in lean companies for the top-down, breakthrough kaizen events, but as time goes on the emphasis of improvement moves to the continuous improvement teams within the value streams. These teams must be within the value streams because they must have view of the entire flow of the processes. This way the focus will always be on improving the flow and increasing the value to the customers; avoiding the pitfall of making local improvement that does not benefit the overall process.

Implementing the Value Stream Organization
The process of attaining a value stream organization follows an orderly progression in synch with the implementation of lean manufacturing. As shown in the figure below, this progression is in three stages. We call the progression a "Maturity Path" because it specifies appropriate steps that can be taken as the company matures in its implementation of lean thinking techniques.

The Maturity Path to Value Stream Organization

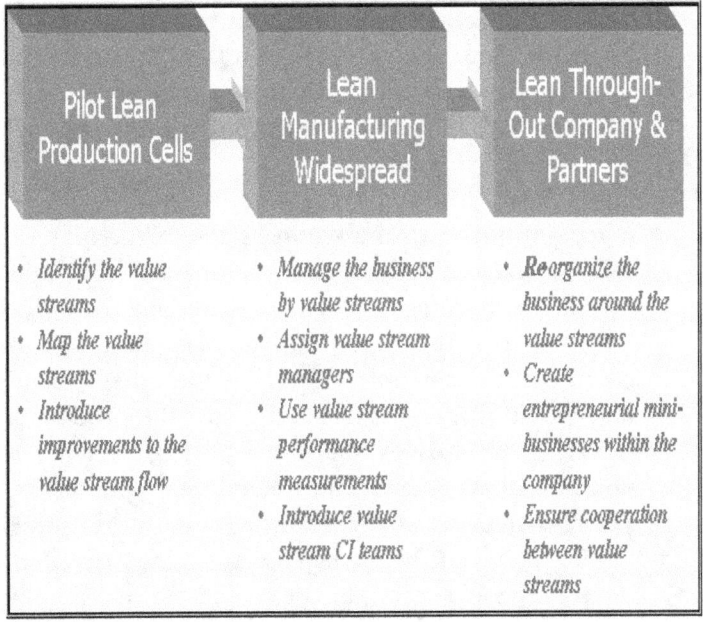

Pilot Lean Production Cells	Lean Manufacturing Widespread	Lean Through-Out Company & Partners
• *Identify the value streams*	• *Manage the business by value streams*	• *Reorganize the business around the value streams*
• *Map the value streams*	• *Assign value stream managers*	• *Create entrepreneurial mini-businesses within the company*
• *Introduce improvements to the value stream flow*	• *Use value stream performance measurements*	• *Ensure cooperation between value streams*
	• *Introduce value stream CI teams*	

The first stage in the Maturity Path occurs when lean manufacturing is being introduced and pilot lean cells are being implemented. The second stage occurs when lean has become widespread in the plant. At this stage it is likely that the cells throughout the plant have been linked into value streams by product group, which cross organizational lines within the plant. The logical next step then is to introduce a value stream organization into the plant. The third stage entails a decision to organize the entire business around value streams. In this stage the value stream becomes the primary organizational scheme, and the departmental structure, if it remains at all, performs a subsidiary role.

It is not necessary to re-draw the company's organization chart in the short term. When lean manufacturing is first being introduced into the company there is no need to make organizational changes. The pilot cells and other lean changes can be achieved without major disruption to the company's departmental structure.

When you move to the second stage of the Maturity Path, it becomes necessary to manage by value stream. In this stage, with lean manufacturing wide-spread across the plant, it becomes important to assign particular people to each of the value streams. This would (ideally) include not only the production people but also support people, such as administration, sales and marketing, purchasing, quality assurance, cost accounting, and all the other people involved in managing the flow of work. Support people need to be dedicated to a value stream in this stage in order to provide the services required to maintain the rate of production. Examples of support functions that need to be more available to a lean value stream are listed below:

Production Control: With the kan-ban as the principal production control mechanism, replacing the work order, there needs be continuous management of the size and number of kan-bans required from the point of view of achieving value stream target rate of production.

Transportation: There need to be personnel responsible for ensuring that the right materials and tooling are at the cells at the time needed to maintain the production flow.

Procurement: There need to be personnel in the value stream responsible for ensuring that materials are received from suppliers in the right quantities and on time.

Manufacturing Engineering: There needs to be engineering support available to ensure the focus on continuous improvement.

Maintenance: There needs to be equipment maintenance personnel available to limit equipment downtime, particularly in a constraint resource.

Assigning people to value streams can be a difficult task. There may be three engineers and four value streams, for example. Or there may be support people with particular specialties required by all value streams. Over the longer term cross-training can bridge these gaps, but in the short term there may be people working in more than one value stream.

Some people worry that a value stream organization will require more people because, for example, there is only one production planner for the factory; yet this work now needs to be incorporated into the value streams. This can be overcome in two ways. First, many of these administrative tasks can be eliminated as lean manufacturing matures within the plant.

Production planning, for example, becomes unnecessary when an effective pull system is in place. Second, cross-training can be used to provide the support department's skills in every value stream. In this scenario, the original production planner joins one value stream and trains people in the other value streams. The production planner, in turn, can be cross trained in inventory control, purchasing, cost reporting, and other support functions. In this way the value streams will contain all the required skills, and no additional people will be needed.

It is common for the department structure to remain in place while the value stream organization is in its infancy. In this case, people still report to their functional bosses, but are assigned to work in particular value stream teams. This matrix management structure is often the most convenient way to make the changes without disrupting the organization of the company. The matrixed organization is most often employed by companies with large and complex operations. They find that their size and complexity makes it more convenient to retain the departmental structure. Having said that, companies that make the radical change quickly are often rewarded by fast and radical improvement. Small and medium-sized organizations almost always take the leap of redrawing the organization chart to reflect value stream management, abandoning their functional organizations.

Once the team is in place and the complexities of the organization have been resolved, the people quickly get focused on increasing value, making improvement, and making more money in their value stream organizations. There are no other departments except for the few people providing support or administrative functions outside of the value streams.

Problems and Issues

Setting up a value stream organization can present difficulties. It is important to keep in mind that it is not necessary to solve all the problems to be able to make progress. It is a lean "rule" that we move ahead step-by-step. If you wait until every eventuality has been discussed and resolved, you will end up doing nothing!! Value streams are like this. Rarely can a "perfect" value stream be set up, but that should not be an obstacle to setting up a good one.

A common question relates to the number of people in the value streams. A useful rule of thumb is that a value stream should contain between 25 and 100 people. If it is bigger than 100 people, it will not have the small-team focus required for the value stream to prosper. If it has less than 25 it will not have enough people to run an effective operation. Although these guidelines have often been successfully violated, they are use points of departure in setting up the value streams for the first time.

A value stream should represent a significant part of the business. Remember, it is in substance a mini-business within the whole. It is important not to have too many value streams. It is common to have three primary value streams, for example, and then have a fourth that contains all the "odds and ends" that don't fit well anywhere else. In establishing the value stream organization, it is useful to keep in mind that it is not necessary to solve all the problems up-front. If you get the three primary value streams working well, you will learn more about the processes and be able to better address the problems as they arise. As products in the fourth value stream become more significant they can be grouped to form a new value stream, or combined into one of the existing ones.

There are always some people within the plant or organization that do not fit into the value streams. These will include:

- People whose work does not apply to any particular value streams. An HR person, for example, or a financial accountant. Other examples would be the plant manager, or the facilities people.
- People who support the value streams but their work is not easily split between each value stream. The IT people who keep the computers running, for example.

- People who do cross-value stream work. It is common to have a QA manager outside the value stream, for example. This person's responsibilities might be to administer the ISO9000 process, certify the training of QA people within the value streams, ensure consistency in quality methods across value streams, and so forth.

The end result is an organization where the majority of people work in the primary value streams, and there are a few vestigial departments supporting the operation. These small departments may be organized in the traditional way, or they may be lumped into a single "cost of doing business" department for budgeting and management purposes.

Chapter 10: Value Stream Implementation

Many companies have pursued lean manufacturing in recent years as a key strategy for profit growth. However, most companies have kept in place traditional measurement and management tools, preventing them from fully realizing the broad benefits of lean. The finance team at one of the companies I use to work for discovered how to unleash the full power of lean through the implementation of a non-traditional approach to measuring and managing the company, called lean accounting.

Lean accounting concepts are designed to better reflect the financial performance of a company that has implemented lean manufacturing processes. These may include methods such as organizing costs by value stream, changing inventory valuation techniques, and modifying financial reports to include nonfinancial information.

Lean manufacturing encompasses a variety of concepts and tools, all aimed at simplification of a business to the essential elements, with an eye to meeting the requirements of the customer in a more effective, and therefore profitable, manner. Lean accounting follows the same mantra as lean manufacturing. Identify value in the eyes of the customer; organize in value streams; apply flow and pull; empower employees; and continually pursue perfection.

Like many companies, we began pursuing lean as a growth strategy for our business a few years ago, using many lean tools to improve operations. As a participant in many kaizen events (focused incremental process improvement projects), the management team knew progress was being made in many areas, yet found it difficult to quantify the improvement using traditional measurements. In fact, some of the financial measures seemed to contradict some of the improvements that had been made, making the team question whether the payoff for the time invested in applying lean practices and tools was worthwhile.

The basic steps we took to pursue Value Stream Management (VSM) included the following:

We identified the main value streams of the company, which included demand creation value streams, new product and business development value streams, and order fulfilment value streams.

We mapped out the key metrics that our company would use to monitor the achievement of the company's main strategies. We identified a set of metrics at the enterprise level, then cascaded the metrics down to the individual division/site, then down to the value stream level and finally down to the cell level. We identified the frequency of the measurements: monthly for certain enterprise and site-level metrics; weekly for value stream metrics; and daily for the cell metrics.

We looked at our processes and followed the guideline that a value stream should comprise between 25 to 150 employees. We organized into three or four value streams per site (one value stream includes members at more than one site); and we developed metric workbooks and supporting value stream financial statements, centred around a one-page summary called a box score, which helped the value stream team monitor their operational, capacity and financial metrics. More than 90% of our employees were assigned to value stream teams, leaving only a small general support group at each site that consisted primarily of functional managers who worked across the value stream teams to improve functional processes. For example, a material excellence leader works to implement kan-ban processes (specific guidelines regarding the frequency, quantities and logistics of parts replenishment) across the order fulfilment value stream.

We changed our chart-of-accounts structure to a few value stream groupings rather than maintaining costs by traditional departments. We maintained a separation of inventoried cost of sales (COS) from that of selling, general and administrative (SG&A) to make end-of-month capitalization of labour and overhead costs simple to identify.

We zeroed out labour and overhead rates from our system and stopped generating and collecting labour and overhead variance information. Like many companies, we found that most of the standard cost and variance information was received too late and involved too many transactions to be of any use in improving our business. We replaced end-of-month variance reports, rarely fully utilized by management, with very visual live hourly and daily operator-generated reporting that is reviewed and acted upon daily by the value stream team. This change contributed to active improvements of production processes.

We split out material costs from other COS conversion costs and used a memo line in our internal financial statements to increase visibility of inventory purchases, which our value stream procurement employees reported on each week.

Challenges

We needed to overcome a few challenges in our day-to-day accounting processes. Traditional functional spending reports no longer exist (that is, HR department spending). Spending is analyzed by value stream instead, and the few functional excellence personnel in the general support group share a "department" in the general ledger. This met with some resistance initially, but the general support group has since realized that they generally do not incur much of the site spending, and the value stream spending is reviewed in detail each week during the value stream metric reviews. This has greatly reduced the number of general ledger accounts used and made forecasting and budgeting much simpler.

Fully burdened standard costs no longer exist. We now maintain material standard costs, based on detailed bills of materials, and value our inventory at the end of the month using a "macro" valuation based on average COS conversion cost per day times the estimated number of days of inventory on hand at the end of the month. This is a very simple calculation that is straightforward and easy to understand and maintain.

VSM has completely changed the way we manage our business. We have a higher level of involvement of employees at all levels and a better understanding of the key drivers of our business and how each employee supports the business. We maintain fewer, but more meaningful, metrics, which are reviewed weekly and really understood and owned by our employees.

When we first began our VSM journey and transferred ownership and accountability of the value stream metrics to the supporting value stream employees, many employees displayed some anxiety because this responsibility had typically fallen to the functional department manager rather than the front-line employees. Most were not used to speaking in front of others from outside their (traditional) functional area. However, it only took a few weekly value stream metric reviews for the various team members to take ownership of their assigned metrics. Metric owners started looking forward to sharing their metric results and leading discussions of trends and root causes of issues they uncovered. It became fun for the metric owners to share the successes they had in improving their metrics.

Similarly, some product management employees were anxious when we announced that we would be zeroing out labour and overhead from standard costs. They were unsure how they would approach decisions regarding things like pricing without such guides. We trained them on decision making under VSM, provided them with some decision-making templates, and reinforced to them that pricing should be market-based rather than cost-plus-based. We also stressed the need to involve the value stream leader in evaluating the impact of the opportunity on the machine and people capacity of the value stream.

Decisions are now made more as a team rather than by function. We have fewer surprises on the production floor as opportunities are no longer "thrown over the wall" from sales and marketing to production before capacity is taken into consideration.

Results

We have strengthened and streamlined our sales and operations planning process, tailoring it to a value stream structure. Our process begins with evaluating the future sales demand, with specific analysis of impact of the demand on available machine and employee capacity as well as the availability of materials to meet the demand. We project the operational, capacity and financial results likely to be generated by the demand and update the projected metrics accordingly. We then meet as a management team to review the issues raised by the projected demand. As a result, we have been able to increase sales volume by more than 15% while increasing return on sales by a similar margin.

We were able to implement the value stream management aspect of lean accounting throughout our facility in a very short time. Part of the success was achieved by engaging our executive management and corporate accounting teams from the start, in the project's design phase. Their understanding of the lean accounting concepts, buy-in to the shared-end vision and assistance in transforming the topside financial statements were extremely helpful.

Chapter 11: Lean Accounting Simplify the Accounting Processes

Transaction elimination

Traditional companies use complex, transaction-based information systems like MRPII or Enterprise Resource Planning Systems (ERP) to maintain financial and operational control of their processes. Lean organizations bring their process under good control using lean methods, visual control, low inventories, short lead times, and most importantly identifying and resolve the root causes of the problems that create the lack of control. Once these root causes have been addressed and the process brought under control, it is no longer necessary to use these complex and wasteful transactional systems, and they can be gradually eliminated.

In manufacturing companies the transaction-heavy documents tend to be production work orders and inventory tracking on the computer. Over time, as lean methods eliminate the need for these documents in favour of visual management, these documents can be eliminated and the thousands of wasteful transaction can be eliminated. One large North American aircraft manufacturer eliminated three trillion transactions in one year using this approach. The "ideal" for a manufacturing company is to have only two types of transactions within the production processes; the receipt of raw materials and the shipment of finished product. These two transactions are legally required owing to change of ownership. Everything else within the production process can be addressed better, quicker, easier, and less wastefully using visual, lean methods.

Other kinds of service companies like banks, healthcare, insurance and others, have similarly transaction-heavy processes that can be radically simplified through the use of lean methods of control. Almost every company can largely eliminate their purchasing and accounts payable processes together with the wasteful and complicated three-way matching through using lean methods.

Accounting controls have always been important, and it is essential that Lean Accounting enhance these controls, and does not weaken them. It is important to bring the company's auditors into the Lean Accounting process at the earliest stages. A primary tool to ensure that Lean Accounting changes are made prudently is the Transaction Elimination Matrix. Using the transaction elimination matrix we can determine what lean methods must be in place to enable us to eliminate traditional, transaction-based processes without jeopardizing financial (or operational) control. These decisions are made ahead of time and become a part of the overall lean transformation; in some cases driving the lean changes and improvements.

Target costing

Target costing is the tool for understanding how the company creates value for the customer and what must be done to create more value. Target Costing is used when new products are being designed and/or when the value stream team needs to understand the changes required to increase the value for the customers. The outcome of this highly cross-functional and cooperative process is a series of initiatives to create more value for the customer and to bring the product costs into line with the company's need for short and long term financial stability. These improvement initiatives encompass sales and marketing, product design, operations, logistics, and administrative processes within the company.

Value-based pricing

The first of the five principles of lean thinking is value to the customer. The prices of products and services are set according to the value created for the customers. Lean accounting includes methods for calculating the amount of value created by a company's products and services, and form that knowledge to establish prices. This approach is in stark contrast to many traditional companies that calculate their prices using the cost-plus method. The cost-plus method establishes prices by calculating a fully absorbed product cost and then adding on an acceptable profit margin. This cost-plus methods leads to serious errors in pricing because it creates a false linkage between price and cost. The price of a product is unrelated to the cost of manufacturing and supplying that product. The price of a product or services is entirely determined by the amount of value created by the product in the eyes of the customers. Lean accounting methods enable value-based pricing.

Chapter 12: Lean Accounting in Lean Manufacturing Environment

Lean manufacturing is nothing new; many manufacturers adopted this business model during the last decade. But did you know that lean accounting is crucial to operating in a lean manufacturing environment? Lean accounting focuses on two goals.

1) Converting financial statements into "plain English,"
2) Eliminating waste by taking the focus off the minutiae.

Standard Costs vs. Lean Accounting Statements

The transparency of lean accounting is helpful in demonstrating the benefits of lean manufacturing initiatives and optimizing day-to-day business operations. Because standard cost accounting rewards overproduction, using standard methods to try to demonstrate the value of lean processes that eliminate production waste would be futile. Lean accounting, on the other hand, reveals savings and costs that might otherwise be misinterpreted or hidden; the true cost of labour and machinery, for example.

For manufacturers that run on lean management principles, not using lean accounting principles can, in fact, be downright harmful. Case in point; standard profit and loss statements can put a negative spin on the inventory reduction that comes with the implementation of lean manufacturing processes. That is because production isn't completely absorbing overhead and labour costs, so these costs appear on statements as deferred costs. This can be a red flag for owners, executives and investors, preventing the benefits of lean manufacturing from shining through.

For example, if a manufacturer produces less product on a quarterly basis, standard cost accounting statements might indicate that the cost of manufacturing each unit goes up because labour and overhead aren't being absorbed as quickly. In other words, standard cost accounting says that the higher a company's production rate, the less each unit cost in terms of labour and infrastructure, as these costs will be divided up among more units. This not only can cause concern among owners, executives and investors, but also can lead manufacturers to price their products inaccurately, making them less competitive. Lean accounting methods, on the other hand, might reveal a lower actual cost per unit, because, in reality, the machines used to make the product are owned by the company and labour costs are minimal.

Lean accounting can avoid this problem by converting financial statements to plain English and using metrics that are clear and objective and support lean initiatives. Deferred labour and overhead costs, for example, have no place on a lean accounting statement. Also, while traditional statements may account for a fixed-dollar/pounds amount of overhead for every dollar/pounds of inventory spent, lean accounting looks at these costs as variable, assessing the true costs of labour and overhead on a case-by-case basis. Statements should also align with value-stream maps visual representations of the end-to-end production process which can give owners and executives a clear picture of their companies' financial situations.

The Lean Lag

While lean accounting provides accurate, easy-to-understand views of finances in lean manufacturing environments, hurdles to acceptance of lean accounting methods remain. Traditional accounting practices are still a compliance necessity because lean accounting won't, for example, satisfy IRS requirements. Likewise, public companies are required to issue financial statements following Generally Accepted Accounting Principles (GAAP), and private companies may have to provide GAAP-compliant statements to lenders. So financials may need to be done twice.

Additionally, lean accounting requires a significant change in the way people think about accounting. Company accountants that know standard cost accounting and GAAP inside and out likely won't be very familiar with lean accounting methods.

Finally, lean accounting requires buy-in from departments outside of finance, including IT, operations, engineering and customer service, because they must all adapt to using lean accounting metrics to measure and analyze performance within their departments.

Is Lean Accounting Right for Your Company?

Even though lean accounting can't replace traditional accounting practices, it can go further in helping owners and executives make accurate, informed business decisions. It is also a necessity for manufacturers who want to see the true financial effects of their lean manufacturing initiatives. Lean accounting may not be right for every organization, but manufacturers that are committed to and invested in lean manufacturing practices should consider supporting them with simplified, lean accounting processes.

Learning Lean Accounting

Traditionally, university accounting programs have shied away from "creative" accounting practices, teaching only Generally Accepted Accounting Principles (GAAP) and standard cost accounting. Lately, however, there is been a perceptible shift in this thinking, and some professors are incorporating lean accounting into their curricula or offering entire courses devoted to the subject.

The Association for Manufacturing Excellence (AME) recently awarded scholarships to 10 students and 10 professors from several universities to attend the organization's annual Lean Accounting Summit. The scholarships were given to those interested in learning how adopting lean accounting principles in their management accounting systems can help organizations make better decisions in their lean transformation efforts.

Even though some universities are taking lean accounting more seriously, roadblocks still exist. University accounting programs aim to groom students for good jobs in the field by placing emphasis on standard accounting, leaving little room for lessons on lean accounting. Lean manufacturers that hope to hire graduates with lean accounting knowledge should work with the universities from which they recruit to encourage professors and university administrators to add lean accounting to curricula.

Chapter 13: Lean Accounting Versus GAAP

The Lean Accounting Profit and Loss statements can be constructed to comply with GAAP with the simple addition of a line at the bottom reflecting the transfer of expenses to the balance sheet in the form of inventory. Firms managing with Lean Accounting typically perform very simple allocations of overheads for GAAP purposes since the only purpose the allocation serves is to comply with GAAP. Often it is as simple as one number for all products.

Many companies choose to run parallel systems, however, performing a monthly reconciliation between the Lean Accounting statements and externally published GAAP compliant statements for the simple reason that they do not want to confuse investors or bankers with the Lean Accounting format. They avoid confusion or resistance to change by maintaining a reconciliation log off-line for purpose of satisfying auditors and assuring compliance. While working from one statement is easier for accounting, either approach is acceptable.

Conversion to Lean Accounting

The transition from traditional management: from a functional organizational structure and traditional accounting to Value Streams and Lean Accounting is best viewed as an ongoing process, rather than a project.

The transition from the old structures to the new can be lengthy and difficult. Often firms have expensive, major pieces of equipment, such as paint systems, heat treat equipment or other 'monument' equipment that must be shared across two or more Value Streams. Such sharing necessitates continuing to allocate the costs of the equipment until such a time as it can be economically replaced with smaller, dedicated machines in each Value Stream.

Similarly, human resources may need to be shared until sufficient cross training can be accomplished. An example might be a company with one buyer and two schedulers that is converting to three Value Streams. The buyer and schedulers will have to be cross trained into three buyer-schedulers, each handling both the buying and the scheduling in a Value Stream.

Finally, management may choose to limit the resources put into the Value Streams until the Value Stream management has climbed the necessary learning curve and can handle some of the more difficult and critical functions. Examples might include new product development or supplier selection, which management may want to keep out of the Value Streams and in their functional area for a matter of months or even years until the Value Streams can manage them effectively.

While the transition is taking place there will be shared resources and shared people, and a degree of allocation of the expenses to the Value Streams will be necessary. This is entire normal and reasonable. Each dedicated resource and each expense that can be directly charged to a Value Stream is a step toward greater accuracy. All that is required is a dedication to continually increasing the resources in the organization assigned directly to Value Streams and continually reducing the percentage of expenses allocated and correspondingly increasing the direct expenses to the Value Streams.

The first five years since the initial Lean Accounting Summit have been exciting ones as the inherent value of structuring accounting in a manner that directly records and encourages manufacturing progress toward the best global practices has become more widely known and adopted. The rate of progress in expanding and improving on the principles and the application has been dramatic. Certainly the next five years will be even more exciting. The leadership role of accounting in the manufacturing transformation to excellence; to lean has come into focus and more and more accounting professionals are embracing the challenge and seizing the opportunity to serve a greater role than simply acting as the record keeper.

Chapter 14: Lean Accounting and Finance Tips for Business

We hear a lot about lean and its use in manufacturing operations. However, lean is a concept that can be used in almost any business and business function. We will focus on operations and understanding their needs in order to produce information critical to run the business.

1. Understand the Value Streams of Your Business: The accounting and finance department serve more internal customers than external customers. In order to provide accurate and timely information for each of the key value streams of a business understanding the needs of those value streams will help to determine what is important for the accounting and finance department. Creating a team that is focused on value and flow or the operations will help accounting and finance to better understand flow from sales to delivery to cash as well as the waste in the process.

2. Simple Weekly Reports: By understanding the value streams, accounting and finance can better determine the reports needed by each value stream to manage the business. Being able to produce quick, meaningful and simple reports will give each value stream better financial control which will allow those value streams to make quicker decisions on spending and flow improvements to ensure sustainable profit margins.

3. Use of Key Performance Indicators (KPI's) or Box Scores: As part of simple weekly reports, producing KPI's or box scores that everyone can agree on will also help to review true performance of value streams. A good KPI report is usually no more than one page with information specific to performance of each value stream. These reports will help each value stream make better decisions when analyzing work flow.

4. Financial Benefits of Lean Improvement: Traditional accounting often shows bad results when good lean change is happening which in turn misleads us about the true impact of lean change. By understanding lean economics; eliminate waste, grow the business, you will be able to better understand the financial and operational benefits of lean for better decision making.

5. Transaction Elimination: All transactions in theory are waste and they cause a lot more waste, but they are required to create financial and operational control. Lean methods and visual management build control into the operational process. When processes are under good operational control, secondary systems are not required. This will allow for the elimination of un-necessary transactions and reporting over time and allow people to focus their time on creating value and improvement instead of driving the system.

Chapter 15: Lean Accounting Focus on the Meaning of Numbers

One of the challenges facing people who want to implement Lean Accounting at their companies is getting buy-in from senior executives. After all, the conventional budgeting process has defined how most for-profit organizations have operated for decades. In the minds of many business leaders, it works.

Lean Accounting is a movement supported by manufacturers and non-manufacturers to completely restructure how accounting is done. This is a by-product of the lean movement. Many companies, public and private, that have become deeply steeped in lean culture have realized that traditional cost accounting is wasteful and, even worse, focuses on the wrong things. Those who live in a truly lean work environment, for instance, know that a fixation on per-unit labour costs (which is extremely common in the manufacturing community) is pointless. Has your customer ever asked what your per-unit labour costs are? Or how much you allocate on a monthly basis for capital costs? Probably not. Yet, the impetus for much action and decision at manufacturing companies is the annual budgeting process followed by re-forecasting throughout the year based on numbers that are time-consuming to reach, rarely reflective of reality, and completely worthless to customers.

Enlightened companies using Lean Accounting have tapped many methods to refocus their accounting systems on creating customer value and collapsing them to reduce waste, such as using rolling forecasts and aligning operations by value stream. No company, however, can start down this path without some executive support. This challenge surfaced again and again in conversations I had with presenters and attendees at the second Lean Accounting Summit held in Orlando in September. A visual workplace is a self-ordering, self-explaining, self-regulating, and self-improving work environment where what is supposed to happen does happen, on time, every time, day or night because of visual solutions.

Shouldn't an accounting system be these things; self-ordering (simple, consistent and not wasteful); self-explaining (so everyone can understand); self-regulating (contributing to/supporting standard process); and self-improving (contributing to/supporting ongoing process improvement)?

This led me to this thought; If an executive understands lean culture, then he or she likely understands the value of symbols in that culture. Once we understood, red bins became much more than just a hard cost that needed to be justified with a return. The bins, which at my former company stored parts, were the fuel of a kanban-based parts-replenishment system that kept inventory low, sent signals vital to pull and flow (which in turn improved flexibility), contributed to level production, made real-time visibility of material flow possible, etc. The invoice that documented the purchase of the bins documented none of these, their most valuable ROI. What if the bins just went away? Perhaps replaced by the replenishment system from before? All of that cost-lowing, customer-value-adding activity would stop.

Flexibility would decrease. Inventory would build. Bottlenecks would become more common because visibility would be clouded. Yet, armed with the wrong number (hard costs only), an accountant might make a bad decision not to buy the bins.

This point could be an opener to a meaningful discussion about conventional accounting versus Lean Accounting because, as I said, numbers are really just symbols. If you don't have the right symbols, you will make bad decisions or worse yet; pass on opportunities to better serve customers through process improvement.

Try this activity. Look at the following list of numbers:
19
1 in 20
902
£1.33
These numbers mean nothing alone. Now consider:

19: The number of women who will serve in the U.S. Senate starting in January 2014.
1 in 20: How many people have congenital heart defects, according to the British Heart Foundation.

902: The estimated number of people executed in China last year, which performed 80% of the world's executions.

£1.33: The cost of a litre of unleaded petrol in London.

Did the numbers themselves tell the story? No, they are symbols for other information that has the power to influence decisions. Should I vote? Should I have my child screened for a heart defect? Should I invest in a politically corrupt country? Should I buy petrol here or in the next town?

Likewise, reviewing your business, which numbers are the most meaningful in terms of giving managers the information that they need to make decisions based on what is happening now to directly please customers? Look at the two things I have emphasized in the last sentence. Because the metrics you choose should meet these two criteria, they will quash the argument that Lean Accounting reduces accountability. If anything, it increases accountability because it shifts the focus to reality and to customers, which erases room to wiggle, hide, fudge and game. If things are not happening as they should, and customers are not getting what they want, flags go up a lot sooner in a Lean Accounting environment than in a conventional accounting environment.

Which brings us back to the reluctant executives. It is entirely possible that these executives don't want the truth to be told. The old system may be serving their personal interests well. This is a difficult situation for sure. The only solace I can offer is that companies that are following the wrong metrics eventually will suffer, and the flags that fly over those mistakes will be hoisted high. This is not hard to see. Just look at what is happening in the auto sector and the increasing interest in Lean Accounting in the healthcare, defence, and even financial sectors. The fever is spreading, just as lean manufacturing started to over 25 years ago.

So it is worth it to at least try to start a Lean Accounting discussion at your company or group. Start with the symbol discussion, which is easy to convey and understand. If it goes nowhere, then start your own effort to determine what metrics should be followed. Then, when warning flags start to fly, you will be in a good position to jump in with a solution.

Chapter 16: Best Practices Cost Accounting Undercuts Lean

Lean manufacturing generally is regarded as a good thing. But when lean fails to integrate accounting, the result can be management reporting that fails to reflect operations improvements and negatively represents lean results. That is not a good thing. Two finance executives who have helped lead lean organizations say it is possible to bridge the operations and accounting worlds and create lean-reflective financials by getting accounting involved in lean initiatives, replacing standard cost-accounting with simpler management reporting and adopting valued-added accounting practices.

The first thing that needs to change in terms of a company's movement toward lean is that the finance executive, the CFO or the controller needs to actually, physically, personally participate in the first kaizen events. We see first-hand that there is real waste being eliminated in the organization; the waste of time, excess inventory and excess activities on the shop floor. Once they see and feel that at some visceral, gut level, they are going to want to make sure that the benefit of that activity is recognizable in their financial statements. In order to make lean recognizable, management reporting needs to move away from cost accounting, which evolved to measure profitability across a range of products and to satisfy generally accepted accounting principles (GAAP) and the Internal Revenue Service.

For example, in a batch-and-queue manufacturer, cost accounting tracks inventory transactions as large batches of material creep from process to process. It identifies the value added to material and attempts to quantify, using time studies and budgeted rates, how much labour and overhead should be absorbed into the financial statement, recording unfavourable variances when production is underutilized. Operations, in response, frequently overproduce one of the "seven deadly wastes" that lean tries to eliminate. In contrast, as a company gets lean, it produces only to customer demand. Cells complete all product processes, cycle times are minutes and inventory is slashed to the quantities moving within cells and quickly to customers. Complex tracking and valuation mechanisms are no longer necessary.

Although you have an inventory valuation that needs to take place for GAAP, you can do it in a much simpler way. A lean manufacturing company I use to work for reduced its inventory from four months to less than four weeks over 3 years. Tracking transactions isn't needed. Once you get to lean, those transactions become waste. Transition Trauma Cost accounting is especially problematic for lean during the financial periods when inventory is being reduced. In a cost-based system, inventory represents, in addition to its material content, "labour and overhead that you incurred to produce the product that you are capitalizing on your balance sheet and deferring the recognition of until some future period when you sell the inventory.

When you go from four months of inventory to three weeks of inventory, all those deferred costs have to come off the balance sheet. There is only one place for those deferred costs to go, and that is through the profit-and-loss (P&L) statement, generally showing up as unfavourable overhead variances. This negative impact alarms unknowing executives, who then question lean initiatives. I think that is why a lot of public companies have a hard time achieving significant success with lean because there is so much emphasis on earnings per share; they don't have the tolerance for this.

To add insult to injury, cost accounting does not clearly show the tangible benefits of lean strategies; improved cash flow, freed-up capacity and reduced floor space. From a management perspective, a standard-cost Profit and Loss is virtually useless. It is not actionable and gives you information that is old and in most cases misleading. Lean companies should create simple-to-read statements that identify "natural" expenses, such as labour, scrap and utilities. Have a financial statement for the company's results for every product line on the first day of the month, every month. Having current information that people understand how to read that can help the organization know how we are doing and what is coming forward. Shareholders and others reading statements need to be educated. Public companies should focus on analysts that cover the company's stock as their first audience because if they don't understand it, they are not going to be able to report it properly in their analytical reports.

Value-Add Accounting: As companies get lean they also reduce material order sizes and increase the frequency of material deliveries. Traditional accounting becomes swamped as it matches packing slips, purchase orders and invoices before paying vendors. Accountants instead should focus on three essentials of material procurement; agree on the price to pay vendors for parts, get vendors to deliver parts on time, and then pay vendors. We found that the cost to control the paper transfer was higher than the cost of the risk that we were incurring by not doing it that way. Reduced tracking and bill-paying activities opens up value-adding opportunities for accounting, such as analysis and consulting.

While we increased inventory turns from four to 10 and more than doubled sales from the same square footage, our accounting staff has shrunk and many outsourced activities, such as tax preparation, were brought in-house. We have improved profitability dramatically, we have improved flexibility, we have more new products being developed, and we have more cash than we ever had. There is no question in my mind that it is because we not only have become a lean manufacturer; we have become lean accountants, lean order management and lean engineers.

Lean Transition: Profits Down, Cash Improved
With cost accounting, the lean transition this fictitious company undergoes shows profits decreasing as deferred labour and overhead hit the statement. What is not nearly as apparent is the lean benefit to cash flow, or cash used, during the period.

Profit: Lean Looks Bad

	Batch & Queue Q1 2002	Lean Transition Q2 2002
Beginning inventory cost	£10,000,000	£10,000,000
Plus Purchased inventory cost	£5,000,000	£2,500,000
Less Ending inventory cost	£10,000,000	£7,500,000
Equal Material costs	**£5,000,000**	**£5,000,000**
Plus Labour costs	£1,500,000	£1,500,000
Plus Overhead costs	£2,000,000	£2,000,000
= Standard costs/Lean costs	**£8,500,000**	**£8,500,000**
+Deferred costs from inventory reductions *	£0	£1,025,000
Plus Cost of goods sold	**£8,500,000**	**£9,525,000**
Sales	£9,000,000	£9,000,000
Less Cost of goods sold	£8,500,000	£9,525,000
Equal Gross profit	**£500,000**	**(£525,000)**

* Percent of total costs (material, labour and overhead) multiplied by inventory reduction. **Cash Used: Lean Looks Good**

Purchased inventory	£5,000,000	£2,500,000
Plus Labour costs	£1,500,000	£1,500,000
Plus Overhead costs	£2,000,000	£2,000,000
Equal Cash used	**£8,500,000**	**£6,000,000**

Chapter 17: Are the Accountants Killing Lean?

Lean must be viewed by everyone in the company as a tool for business growth, not just cost control.

When manufacturing managers first embraced lean in the early '90's it was the doubting accountants who had to be dragged along, demanding guarantees for the return on investment that just were not available at the time. While manufacturing professionals were quick to see Lean as a powerful new philosophy for meeting customer demand, the accountants often saw it as just another buzz word and an opportunity to spend money on consultants. Reorganizing the factory floor for flow was not cheap and without a lot of evidence that the costs would be recouped, the accountants were understandably reluctant.

The evidence is now in and Lean has proved itself to be a money maker. Everyone gets it, even the accountants. And there is the danger. Where the manufacturing engineer sees the beauty in efficient flow resulting in ever greater throughput, the accountant sees the same transformation of the factory as a direct path to the reduction of production costs. They are both right, but when the concept of Lean Thinking is reduced to a euphemism for cost reduction then the opportunity for sustained continuous improvement is threatened. The manufacturing leader needs to keep the entire team focused on Lean as the path to long term growth if he is to reap sustained benefits.

Any Lean-trained manufacturing expert can walk through a pre-lean factory and point out lean-like recommendations; shorter component travel here, smoother flow there, Kanbans, or whatever. Once implemented, these suggestions reduce labour hours and, in fact, do produce quick payback. The consultant gets paid, the accountants' doubts are suspended and all but the laid off employees seem happy. So management calls for more of the same.

Sure enough, the consultant is brought back in. Kaizans are held, the factory is reorganized again, cost reductions are tallied and the management team celebrates the savings. But this time the savings are only half again as large as the first round. And then the accountants notice that costs are not continuing to go down. In fact, despite yet another round of Kaizens, costs are slowly beginning to rise. Their doubts come back and they question the Manufacturing team as to why they should continue to fund Lean initiatives. The management team begins to lose interest in Lean.

As in the example above, Lean is often equated with cost cutting and one hears talk such as, "Our costs are way too high, we need to get lean." Management teams are aware of success stories from other companies, and maybe remember the progress made during their own prior forays into Lean, and believe that if they were only to redouble their efforts they could really make an impact on cost.

Next thing you know, the boss announces a new "lean program" that will "really cut costs to benchmark levels" The accountants come up with cost reduction targets for manufacturing. The management team rallies behind the boss and they roll out the Lean program to the rank and file. And the rank and file yawns and dusts off their resumes. They have seen Lean work before, and to them it is just another word for lay-off.

For Lean to become an effective and sustaining way of doing business, the following attributes are required:

- **Seen by all as a tool for business growth, not just cost control:** Management must structure the Lean program around long term growth objectives, more rewarding jobs and as the best path to job security.
- **Workers trust the management team:** Begin with a commitment to not lay off workers who find ways to eliminate their jobs. If trust is already low, start small. Early successes in waste reduction are celebrated and rewarded. Expand the program as trust improves.
- **The management team trusts the workers:** Muda reduction ideas are funded without undo justification. Don't demand ROI charts from work teams.
- **Program is bottom-up energized, not top down driven:** Workers will self-sustain programs that benefit them personally. Once they see the waste, they will choose to

eliminate it themselves if the result leads to more rewarding work.

- **Use consultants to train others to see, not to identify waste themselves:** Nobody can see waste as well as those doing the task.
- **Lean techniques are applied across the enterprise, not just in manufacturing:** Why do only blue collar workers harbour Muda? They don't, so don't send that message. The opportunities are equally great in engineering, and yes, even accounting.

But what about the company that is barely surviving in a downward turning market? With little hope of gaining new business, the management team feels they need to cut costs just to survive. In this case, bring in the experts, cut where they recommend and do your lay-offs as you see fit. But just don't call it Lean. Because if and when the business does turn around, and you want to implement Lean to free up workers so you can apply them elsewhere, it will be too late. Lean Thinking will be forever tainted by the cost cutting brush. If you must lay off workers, then lay them off first and introduce Lean sometime thereafter. Or implement Lean cautiously and claim savings at the rate that freed up labour can be absorbed elsewhere in the enterprise. Then use Lean to find ways to get the same work done with the fewer people you now have.

So how do you know when your Lean program is healthy?

Here are a few signs:

1. **Workers volunteer to be on Kaizen teams, both blue collar and white:** White collar buy-in to Muda reduction will be a harder sell than blue collar. Bigger egos don't want to accept the idea that they are producing waste. Begin with white collar Lean.

2. **Savings from Kaizen round two are even greater than round one:** Now that the Kaizen teams trust the leadership they will be even more adept at identifying and extracting Muda.

3. **Workers request Lean training:** They see it as job enrichment and the opportunity to participate in a process that has management interest and favour.

4. **Lean terms like "Muda," "Kaizen" and "Flow" are part of the company's vocabulary:** It becomes an intrinsic tool of business as usual.

5. **Employees are leading Kaizen events, not consultants:** Lean is a basic job skill, not a specialist task.

6. **Learning curves are beating expectations:** Lean results tend to expand across an organization and reap unexpected savings. Cheaper, better, faster ideas spread quickly to operations not yet "leaned out."

7. **Quality is improving:** Fewer operations, less travel and reduced labour input all result in fewer opportunities for error. Errors themselves are Muda and will be attacked directly.

8. **Costs are continuously declining:** There is no end to cost reduction and the opportunities do not dry up. Every time a process is opened up for scrutiny; new opportunities to extract Muda are seen.
9. **Business is growing:** Lower costs and better quality from a more engaged and satisfied workforce almost always leads to higher customer satisfaction and a more successful business.

Chapter 18: Lean Accounting's Fat Problem

There is an obscure accounting battle bubbling up around the world that has broad implications for how to run a business. The battle begins when a company starts to implement "lean manufacturing," a practice that pits costs against productivity.

This chapter examines the implications of the way lean philosophy asks companies to rethink their businesses starting with basic principles.

Lean, in the simplified form, involves three fundamental concepts; flow, pull and continuous improvement. The idea of flow is that manufacturing processes should operate as a continuous flow with as few interruptions as possible. In lean parlance, flow processes are called value streams and they run counter to the departmental and functional silos that dominate the organisational charts of most companies. The generalization of lean has taken this paradigm and applied it to processes outside of manufacturing such as health care, financial services and construction.

The idea of pull is that manufacturing should occur in response to actual demand, not predictions about inventory. A pull system is used to organize functions when the flow process is initiated. Instead of making products based on predictions and forecasts, you make them when an order is received.

The idea of continuous improvement is that there should be a constant and never-ending effort to reduce waste and improve productivity. Individual employees in an organization must be encouraged and made responsible for finding improvements and empowered to implement changes.

So in a lean process, the demand signals pull the materials through the flow processes and the right number of products is created with as little waste as possible. When all the suppliers of materials are also making their processes lean, the result is that the entire supply chain is extremely responsive and efficient. One of the biggest benefits of lean is that it allows companies to dramatically reduce their cycle times, that is, the amount of time from getting the order to delivering the product. This happens when the flow processes are redesigned to eliminate delays. Implementing lean also usually means a company can make significant reductions in inventory.

Here is where the accounting fun begins.

If I have £100 of inventory and I reduce it by £80, everyone should be happy, right? The company now has less money tied up in inventory and that money can be used for other purposes. But unless you understand the big picture, when you start to implement lean practices, it looks like they cost you money. Why? An £80 reduction in inventory is a loss from the financial perspective if you handle it as a write off and profits go down. You did have a higher level of inventory and now you have a lower level. That £80 reduces your shareholder's equity, although it is really a benefit. (Note to accounting experts: This is a simplistic case that represents the problem people are having in the field. We could argue all day about different ways to approach accounting for this inventory.)

Unless the accountants understand the way that lean works, in the worst case it seems to them that lean produces losses, not efficiencies. In a typical case, they cannot see the cost advantages. This is the source of many of the arguments I found out about at the Lean Enterprise Summit.

The people attending the summit, those who were fighting to introduce lean into their companies, reported over and over again that finding a way to reconcile accounting the way lean does it and standard cost accounting was proving to be much harder than it should be.

Lean practitioners think of accounting in cash terms. Lean is against creating data and reports for their own sake. That would be considered another form of waste. In general, lean advocates have a jaundiced view of enterprise software and any general-purpose automation tools. The lean approach measures how well your value stream is working.

One presenter at the summit used weight loss as an analogy. When dieting, standard cost accounting would advise you to weigh yourself once a week to see if you are losing weight; Lean accounting would measure your calorie intake and your exercise and then attempt to adjust them until you achieve the

115

desired outcome. While this analogy is oversimplified, it does get to the core difference between lean and standard cost accounting. Lean accounting attempts to find measures that predict success. Standard cost accounting measures results after the fact. But even when the accounting types and the lean practitioners start to understand each other, problems remain. How can we reconcile the kind of data collection and accounting that lean demands and the standard cost accounting? Duplicated data collection and reporting is indeed a form of waste.

Value stream accounting was suggested by a colleague of mine as a way out. The company's revenues and costs are reported weekly for each of the value streams. The costs reported do not include allocations or standard costs, just the costs that actually occurred within the value stream last week. This produces reports that are easy to understand and are used for cost control; they also monitor the cost reductions or profit increases coming from the company's lean improvements. This report also gives the information needed for making routine business decisions. In some cases it is possible to implement value stream accounting using profitability and cost management systems that allow advanced modelling of costs in a way that still connects everything to the chart of accounts and shared cost allocations used in standard cost accounting.

One presenter explained that when financial cost-focused accounting was adopted in the U.S. about 100 years ago, its promoters warned that it would not be a good tool for operational management. A growing body of experience at companies implementing lean accounting is showing that they were right. Too many vital decisions are based on standard cost accounting, which obscures the true operational picture.

Chapter 19: Why and How Lean Accounting Works

Successful lean accounting involves providing simple, transparent, and meaningful information for organisations' needs.

Organisations across industries and with varying business models are adopting and implementing customer-focused lean strategies. This type of strategy transforms an organisation by pushing decisions down within the business, standardising processes to build in efficiencies and quality, embracing a focus on continuous improvement, and empowering the employees. But such a change in delivery system necessitates changes in support areas, such as purchasing and even accounting.

Why must accounting information change?

The goal of management accounting information is to provide the necessary data and information for decision-making. There are three key reasons why this information must change in a lean environment.

The goals of the system have changed

The goal of a traditional system is increased efficiency and lower cost per unit. Consequently, manufacturing in larger batches is encouraged because this means fewer changeovers and lower prices on material, leading to lower costs. Yet batch processing does not consider the hidden costs of inventory movement, storage, obsolescence and damage. Even service and support areas process batches of reports, invoices, etc. The real cost, however, is the lack of flexibility and the increased working capital that processing in large batches requires.

The primary focus of a lean system is not on reducing the cost per unit, but on creating and managing smooth, high quality, and efficient processes. The goal is to produce and deliver 100% quality products and services, in a smooth flow and on time. This is done by focusing on constantly improving processes and shortening lead times so that flexibility and capacity increase without large capital investments. Working capital requirements decrease as the order to invoice time reduces. The overall effect is improved cost efficiency.

The organisational structure has changed

Traditionally managed organisations are vertically structured with department managers responsible for decision-making and budget accountability. Accounting reports comparing actual spending with pre-designed budgets have therefore been targeted towards these managers. Lean organisations are more horizontal. Cross-functional value stream teams are now responsible for most operational decisions. A value stream encompasses all resources and people involved in a process from beginning to end. One example of a value stream team would be an order fulfilling value stream whose process is to produce and deliver current products to customers. This value stream includes not only machine operators, but also forklift drivers, setup personnel, purchasing agent, and even an accountant. In other words, anyone and any resource directly involved in the planning, production and movement of product. Another example could be a new product development value stream. In this case, team members would probably include marketing, designers, CAD engineers, process and mechanical engineers and an accountant. It makes sense that accounting information targets the value stream teams rather than functional departments and managers that are no longer relevant.

The timing of information needs has changed

Accounting is a transactional control system designed to provide summaries of activities to managers so that they can assess whether or not their areas were (over the given period) 'in control'. In other words, variance reporting in the form of departmental expense reports and profit and loss reports indicates whether their area met expectations as defined by the annual budget. Reporting is reliant on accounting cycles and is, therefore, monthly. By this time, the magnitude of the problem is usually large because it was not caught and communicated right away.

In a lean system, value stream teams need to know right away when the process is 'out of control'. Visual management is a critical element of any lean system because it alerts all users immediately to the status and needs of the process crucially, in time to make corrections before more problems occur. Visual management may take the form of lights signalling when a machine is down, a metric board where cell team members track the days' production, on-time-delivery and quality results, or even a well-placed computer monitor that allows employees to easily track progress. Visual management reduces time wasted looking for information and the potential danger of not knowing when a change needs to occur. For these three reasons organisational structure, decision authority, and timing in order to become 'lean' it is critical to address the accounting information currently provided in our organisations to determine its relevancy.

What is the essence of lean accounting?

The key to successful lean accounting is providing simple, transparent and meaningful information for given recipients' needs.

Chapter 20: The Impact of Lean Accounting in Organizations Today

Business owners often use accounting to make business decisions and improve their company's operations. Management accounting is a primary internal function companies use to manage production processes. Management accounting is the internal function that allocates costs, creates budgets and forecasts production output. Lean accounting is a revolutionary accounting process that transforms current accounting functions. Lean accounting focuses on creating short production cycles and producing products that meet immediate consumer demand. Lean accounting impacts companies in several different ways.

Reduce Waste

Lean accounting focuses on reducing waste in a company's production process. Reducing waste can help companies improve their overall profitability. This is a significant impact, because companies that can maintain or increase production output use less business capital. These companies can then reinvest saved capital into the business and make additional improvements in the production process. Business owners may also find that reducing waste can improve the quality of their products and the company's public image.

Improve Efficiency

Business owners can use lean accounting to improve employee efficiency. Improving efficiency often allows companies to produce the same amount of goods or services with fewer employees. This is a significant benefit, as labour cost is usually the highest expense in the company, and finding ways to reduce labour will ultimately save money. Efficiency improvements can also create a competitive advantage in the business environment. A competitive advantage allows businesses to produce goods or services better than other similar companies in the economic marketplace.

Retrain Employees

Retraining employees can have a positive or negative impact from lean accounting. Lean accounting can help current employees learn new skills to improve their knowledge in production systems. This knowledge creates a more skilled worker for the company. However, lean accounting requires business owners to be educated in this function or use an outside professional to retrain employees. Business owners may find that management accountants are reluctant to accept lean accounting principles, since it is a newer accounting concept with mixed reviews in the business environment.

Profitability Issues

Lean accounting often distorts the pricing process for individual goods or services. Indirect costs usually represent the general and administrative expenses of the company. Price distortion is the result of lean accounting failing to consider the indirect costs of production processes. Companies may find they have a difficult time maintaining profitability when using lean accounting due to this issue. Examples include office facilities, sales staff and administrative workers completing back-office functions.

Cost Increases

Lean accounting can also increase the company's overall operating costs. The concept of lean accounting emphasizes speed and quality regardless of cost. Companies may need new production equipment to achieve lean accounting waste reduction and efficiency goals. However, the equipment may result in an unmanageable upfront expense for businesses who are not sure if lean accounting will provide long-term benefits. Business owners may also face higher implementation and maintenance costs for new equipment, which can reduce the benefits of lean accounting.

Chapter 21: Accounting for What Happened

In deciding where to produce products, Total Cost of Ownership, gives companies an accurate insight into the lifecycle of costs.

Manufacturers are reinvesting in U.S. to more efficiently serve the world's largest free market. That is why they are back. They are not returning on an impulse or because of public pressure. But unlike when they left, this time they are measuring why they should return.

Let me be clear; when it comes to the reshoring debate, I am an cynic. I believe in numbers. And while not everything in business can be perfectly quantified, numbers help separate emotion and impulse from fact.

Evidence is mounting from surveys and direct statements by leading manufacturers, such as GE and Ford, that the flow of U.S. production overseas is levelling off and that domestic production is on the rise. There is a lot of emotion being generated about this, as there was when companies departed our shores. There is also some mystery and uncertainty about why this trend is actually happening and if it can be sustained.

I can say with confidence that most manufacturing companies that left the U.S. with a goal to ship products back did not do much offshore accounting. They based their decisions largely on favourable piece-part costs (from low-detail bids) and on cheap, unburdened foreign-labour rates.

What they encountered offshore was an indirect labour burden of five-to-one; constant turnover, training costs and wage hikes; escalating shipping fees and an impaired asset base back home.

Travel and other expenses were hidden in corporate budgets and were never placed on the piece part that first drew them to foreign soil.

Once their overheads started to skyrocket and operating profits plunged, however, those companies felt the "real" math like a stomach virus.

The lesson; even if you choose not to practice Total Cost of Ownership (TCO), your company will live or die by it anyway. So better do TCO with the joy of playing a favourite board game, or watch your profits tumble and competitors step ahead.

Using Total Cost of Ownership (TCO) in Decision-Making

For us, Total Cost of Ownership is the sum of the piece part, associated logistics and all of the soft costs inclusive of the decision to source an item into a specific geography. (In our growing markets, that means Taiwan, China and the U.S., equally.)

We never debate "offshoring" against "reshoring" or "in-shoring," although we quantify and act on geographic risk when protecting our intellectual property. We are numbers-driven. What we are doing because the numbers generally point us in this direction is Build Where You Sell.

Build Where You Sell is what is increasingly happening in America and elsewhere. This is the essence of what Reshoring is. Seen in this light, it will be much easier to accept the new math of TCO, whether you are a company or a nation setting policy.

Back to explaining our plan; we are expanding our definition of TCO to include not only the physical length of the ultimate supply-to-demand fulfilment line, but also the associated lead times of the entire process. That is order-to-cash complete, full explosion of the Bill of Materials (and suppliers' BOMs) in order to understand the total amount of time it takes to respond to a demand signal and the total amount of material liability within the supply pipeline.

We believes that, just as we try to shorten the demand-fulfilment chain, we should also shorten the overall lead-time of the supply fulfilment change. This will result in more operating profit. It will also lead to better management of that operating profit because we won't have to invest as much in inventory; why – because lead time is a component of all replenishment systems, whether it is safety stock, min-max, Kanban or eKanban.

If all this sounds like a regionalization "reshoring" pitch; it is. Currently, regional manufacturing and distribution is the quickest way to fulfil demand while minimizing risk. We are always striving to get closer to the customer and in many of our instrumentation markets speed of delivery is the order winner.

Our goal is to be the most responsive business within the most cyclical markets, and to deliver the exact price and quality the market needs. This takes a concerted effort to reduce part count, "right-tolerance," select commercial off-the-shelf (COTS) materials and components when they perfectly match requirements, lean the organization, do TCO, and more!

Why did I speak earlier about the integrated team? And what is the secret sauce to ending the silos between design and procurement?

TCO gives a company hard insight into the lifecycle of costs. There is a ledger that starts and ends with decision-enriching numbers. It helps one see the organization as a whole. But what is even more startling is the impact that robust product design has on operating profit and efficiency in every upstream department. Like the hidden costs that damaged the offshore movement, there are hidden efficiencies from a numbers-driven design effort that ignite cascading and far-reaching benefits.

Chapter 22: Lean Accounting Implementation

Steps to simplify cost management and improve profitability by confronting shop floor reality while still satisfying GAAP

If you use a shop floor management system, you are familiar with the frustration of trying to use job tracking reports to improve the bottom line. These reports are retrospective in nature, meaning that they give a snapshot of costing data after the deeds are done, usually in less than user-friendly language. They imply that you can manage manufacturing processes by analyzing job cost accounting numbers and reviewing the results.

So, you show the numbers to supervisors hoping for improvement to be gained from insights gleaned from the reports, but that improvement is often elusive. Trends seem inconsistent from one period to the next with no real improvement in profitability. Global competitive pressures keep a tight lid on the extent to which price increases can help, so you probably find yourself asking what can I do on the shop floor to protect and improve profitability?

Well, the answer is simple and direct - Confront Reality. What do I mean by reality? The reality is that managing by results does not work in a lean organization and never has. To effectively manage profitability in a lean company, you should reconsider this management practice now; before it is too late and consider implementing lean accounting practices that reflect the working reality of your shop floor. For managers who have experienced the transformative power of lean improvements, it should come as no surprise that it takes lean thinking to profitably manage a lean enterprise.

Leveraging the Lean Advantage

Why does managing by results not work in lean organizations?

It's simple; most supervisors, let alone operators and other shop personnel do not understand what the numbers on tracking reports signify. To satisfy Generally Accepted Accounting Principles (GAAP), your company is likely using some sort of allocation processes or variances to make the numbers comprehensive. This is done to ensure that the cost data are representative of the complete or total cost of operations. But for shop personnel (let alone cost accounting professionals), the reports end up distorting what has happened in the manufacturing process to the extent that it is not recognizable to them in a meaningful way. In short, it does not reflect the reality they observe and work in every day, making it virtually impossible for your shop people to react with corrective measures that will drive better results. Okay, point made, you say, "but what can I do?"

What you can do is introduce Lean Accounting Methodology throughout your company. To understand what lean accounting can do for your business, let's first take a look at what accounting in general is all about.

Accounting is nothing more than tracking inflow to outflow as a measure of profitability, which is governed by GAAP. Essentially, GAAP-driven accounting methods provide the "10,000-foot view" of the financial operations of a company. As these methods proliferate across the company and throughout the manufacturing process with sophisticated allocation and job-costing practices, complexity increases and everyday decipherability usually decreases. Lean Accounting Methodology simplifies and streamlines the accounting process without upsetting GAAP by replacing distorting, confusing and time-wasting parts of the process with metrics and analysis that is grounded in the language of the lean manufacturing processes-the "value stream flow process" that you and your people have already successfully implemented.

The Simple Logic of Lean Accounting

As the implementation of lean processes expands throughout the organization, the principles of traditional accounting theory become ineffective as a management tool. This is because the traditional approach is retrospective in nature (management by results) and tries to "steer from the back end of the process." This is wholly contradictory to the prospective, forward-looking nature of lean methodology. In the lean organization, value stream processes require a new take on management cost

133

accounting, driving a new concept of "Management by Means" or "Management at the Point of Action." In the transition to lean accounting practices, traditional accounting practices GO AWAY: they are removed from operations or value stream flows.

In traditional financial accounting, data about labour, equipment, material, etc. enters the operational value streams (Inflow) and finished products exit the other side of those streams. These two data points can be sent through the 10,000 foot view of the financial accounting system to generate income statements and otherwise satisfy GAAP requirements. But this financial information never enters the operation/value streams. The question on every business executive's or owner's mind is how do we measure what happens in value streams and operations?

The Logical Answer

Admit that traditional cost accounting methods do not and cannot accurately and appropriately measure operational activity in lean organizations based on the value stream concept.

The underlying principles that guide lean implementation and the creation of value streams are flow, self-improvement and problem resolution. These principles must also be the foundation for properly designed, well executed and continually improving lean accounting systems.

Focus on what is happening from moment to moment inside value stream operations using metrics that reflect lean practices and values in plain language and understandable analytics.

Value Stream Costing simplifies the accounting process to give everyone real information in a basic, understandable format. By isolating all fixed costs, value stream costing identifies the resources (direct labour, materials, supplies, etc.) consumed in the value stream. Costs represented in this way are easily applied to a given Value Stream through metrics that are accessible and understandable to the shop personnel who work every day in the cells or stations that make up the value streams.

Beyond the representation of direct manufacturing costs, any operating cost that can be effectively apportioned to a value stream, such as rent, utilities, or machinery expense, can be easily applied to value streams as a commonly understood value. People intuitively understand the nature of these costs from everyday life and can easily associate them with the space used in manufacturing processes that make up a value stream. For example, a metric representing these costs on a basis of the square footage utilized by a particular workstation is easy to grasp.

Such a factoring methodology when broadly applied can provide a truer picture of workstation cost consumption relative to value-added throughput for each value stream company-wide. As an example, if a workstation is found to include unused floor space that might be released for use in another value stream process, reducing the shop space utilized by the stream would correspondingly reduce the associated square-foot apportioned operating costs, while making way for better, more profitable use of the space in another value stream.

This approach to value stream costing is really a transition process that is completely dependent on a focused corporate vision; moving from Management by Results to Management by Means or at the Point-of-Action. The goal is a simplification of management accounting practices that focuses on what is actually happening at any given moment in the operations within value streams in a lean company. This means designing metrics that reflect and measure manufacturing activity according to the lean values at the foundation of the company.

In today's lean world, one company stands out-Toyota. At Toyota, the guiding management vision is expressed through their "True North" metrics, which include growing the skills of the workforce, enhancing the quality of products, reducing the cycle time of production, and building profitability through productivity and cost management. These four key areas of Toyota's True North metrics drive comprehensive, company-wide lean improvement efforts while still hitting all of the crucial figures on corporate financials. It is an example to be emulated and followed.

Chapter 23: Lean Accounting Implementation Case Study

One of the Companies we work with in Wiltshire area of the United Kingdom is a state-of-the-art precision machining job shop serving the High Tech, Automotive, medical and aerospace markets. Over a number of years, the managing Director Andy Jones, developed a custom computerized shop floor data collection system to track and gather data from their traditional job costing and work flow processes.

Constantly seeking improvements in manufacturing methodology, Mr. Jones and his management team began implementing Lean Manufacturing practices in 2010. An intense kaizen event was staged for the purpose of value stream mapping the in-house work order data collection process. Representatives from business partner companies, outside consultants as well as company management and shop floor personnel participated in the rigorous review.

The outcome was a much clearer understanding of the value stream flows within the company and the decision to unplug the custom shop floor data collection system. Analysis clearly showed that it was too costly, time consuming and inaccurate a tool to support critical management business decision-making. Jones's experience at the helm of the company had taught him that misleading data can result in disastrous management decision making. Reflecting on the insights revealed by several kaizen events, his team decided to develop, test and implement a "Kanban" work order card system that has proven to be a dramatic success and the company was well on its way to becoming a fully Lean company.

In 2012, Mr. Jones and his team participated in the start-up of the Lean Accounting SIG (special interest group) in conjunction with us, (AA Global Sourcing Ltd). The purpose of the Lean Accounting SIG was to facilitate learning about lean accounting principles, methodologies and implementation strategies among business associates advocating lean manufacturing principles.

Through AA Global Sourcing Ltd, I contacted Jones because I was interested in what topics the group was working on. Learning of the group's interest in studying lean accounting issues, I generously offered to loan my thesis "A Lean Accounting System For Manufacturing Companies" to the group for continuing study.

While familiarizing himself with my ideas and doing background research into related issues, Jones became familiar with my work and my theory of reducing overhead expenses to direct costs or "production factors" as they relate to, or are consumed in, the manufacturing process. My theory describes a single piece flow where each machine in a manufacturing process continually produces a single component of the product and the output of all the machines in the larger product flow are coordinated to ensure the most rapid assembly of the finished product possible.

The implication for manufacturing was a flexible approach to managing labour, raw materials and production machinery that would allow for their most efficient use in manufacturing any given product. I believed that manufacturers should maintain an inventory of raw material that was just sufficient to support the flow of production, and advocated a cycle of customer orders and production where product was sold and delivered as fast as it was manufactured.

Jones recognized something very familiar in my views. The parallels with the value stream concept that he was implementing in his company were very strong, but it was obvious to Jones that his company confronted two limiting factors.

First, as a custom "job shop", the composition of production flows; the value streams would change based on the unique type of product that customers actually ordered.

Second, it was not feasible for his company to constantly reposition the large and heavy machinery in the shop to accommodate optimized flow.

Jones knew that to implement a truly lean methodology, he would have to take a hard look at work practices, categorizing all effort by processes and developing families of parts with similar flow characteristics.

This approach would allow his company to organize or group machines for processing the particular family of parts in a hybrid flow process, eliminating wasted movements and lag time waiting for availability of the next process.

After intensive analysis, review and internal process modelling, the team developed six distinct value streams at the core of manufacturing operations:

Value Stream Description	Colour Code
550 CNC Horizontal 3 machine Cell System	Red
500 CNC Horizontal 3 machine Cell System	Purple
CNC Horizontal and Vertical Milling Machines	Blue
CNC Turning Centers with live tooling and Robo Drills	Yellow
Auto Band Saw, CNC Turning laths and Horizontal Mill	Orange
Fixturing, Tooling, Maintenance & Shipping / Receiving	Green

The colours associated with the individual value streams are for the purpose of quick visual identification of activities, resources, metrics and performance measures unique to particular value streams. Colour-coding also enable quick, intuitive and easy matching of other lean processes to a particular value stream. For example, colour-coding Kanban cards to particular value streams facilitate easy match-up of costs to the area of consumption, and colour-coded work-orders clearly identify the value streams they belong to. The company is also extending the colour-coding schema to work-force assignments, purchasing and inventory, as well as customer sales, service and shipping. The simple visual aid of colour is helping the team to fully integrate value stream costing practices throughout the enterprise

In a perfect "lean world" of manufacturing, employees would consistently be on target for takt-time and daily process improvements-right. But in the imperfect world where today's lean manufacturing actually takes place, management needs a means of reliably gauging the shop floor reality in support of tactical as well as strategic business decision making. Reflecting on this problem-how to collect valid production data for decisive management action. Jones came full circle to the problem he encountered in the old custom shop management software application he had originally created for the company. How could he see what is really happening within the value stream processes if the information he was receiving about the bottom line was in disarray? It became apparent to him that accounting in a Lean manufacturing environment was going to require the creation of appropriately lean financial reporting and management tools.

The team set to the task of developing value stream costing practices. They identified the resources that were consumed in each value stream and devised factors to represent them that were easily understood by supervisors and operators on the shop floor. To present data gathered from resource factoring in the value stream, they devised a "plain English" profit and loss statement.

141

Brainstorming over how resource factoring might be broadened to include some of the fixed costs traditionally represented in company overhead, Jones hit upon the idea of using the square footage of production space in the shop dedicated to a value stream as a basis for applying resource factoring. Any cost that could be effectively and accurately apportioned over the entire shop space (utilities, rent, facilities and equipment maintenance, etc.) could be allocated through resource factoring in the same common sense, plain English way as materials, effort and equipment utilization.

Wanting a straightforward way of presenting lean accounting metrics to shop personnel that did not require the ability to wade through complex financial statements, They went on to develop a "Box Score Card" that quickly and easily portrayed cost and performance metrics for daily, weekly, monthly, quarterly and yearly reporting periods. The box score card provides direct visual feedback utilizing colour coding for easy recognition of daily, weekly or monthly metrics, performance and target values as a reference for further improvement.

To formalize the lean accounting methodology they were creating, Jones decided to take another stab at developing software to support efficient and effective cost management in lean organizations. Jones is automating many of these ideas and processes and incorporating them in a new generation of lean software tools that help lean organizations systematically identify and remove waste and

142

production inefficiencies. Ultimately Jones's goal is to share these innovations through distribution of a suite of software tools that will make the lean accounting transition easier for others than it has been for him.

Since the development of software tools for lean accounting cost management is still in its infancy, measurement of its effectiveness over the long range will require continued development, testing and real-world application. But the interim results of the overall effort to effect a lean transition at Jones company are impressive and promising. As a part of their value stream costing methodology, they created a Lean Productivity Index (LPI) metric that measures value-added sales throughput in hours monthly per employee. Over the past three years of progressive lean implementations in the company's operations, that metric has seen an improvement from 96.32 hours per employee in 2009 to 188.78 hours per employee in 2010.

Jones feels that the truth is in the improving performance and productivity numbers. Says Jones, "Our company today is decidedly a constantly improving lean machine."

The hard facts of a changing manufacturing reality mean introducing lean accounting methodology throughout your organization. Continuing traditional accounting practices risks derailing the lean organization you have laboured to create. In today's highly-competitive global marketplace the consequences can mean downsizing due to loss of profitability or even to the point of bankruptcy.

The choice is yours and only yours.

Chapter 24: Best Practices for Implementation

Based on my experience at various companies I use to work for, I offer these tips and best practices for successfully implementing value stream management, or lean accounting, at your company.

Upper management support is critical: Without that, it will surely fail. The changes that will ensue, and the subsequent effects to your reporting methodology, will be significant, and if you do not have buy-in from your controlling entity, you will spend much more time trying to maintain two reporting structures and also trying to explain why certain results are happening.

Everyone must understand that lean is a growth strategy not a cost-cutting strategy: The true power of lean is to flow more product through your plant with the same resources more efficiently with less waste at higher profits. This is also why product management and your sales team needs to be solidly linked to your value stream. They will be the pillars of your organization to drive the increased sales.

Properly identify your value streams: You really need to analyze your products by the product families, the processes they go through and how they flow through your plant. Create value streams as close to your suppliers and customers as possible. Make sure to include your marketing and customer-facing functions, as they "are critical to the concept of a complete value stream.

Don't try to attain perfection before setting up your value streams: You will never get there, so spend an adequate amount of time understanding your products and their flow through the facility. Lean manufacturing emphasizes continuous improvement; likewise, you should constantly revisit, rearrange and improve your value streams.

Keep metrics and methods simple and manual in the beginning: We had multiple existing metrics, and the natural response is to try to duplicate the metrics. This would be a mistake. First of all, many of the metrics could be driven off the old standard cost system. They also could be based on pre-lean thought processes, which would cause confusion and frustration within the value stream and from the corporate level. Also, trying to measure too many metrics could be counterproductive to removing waste.

Do not set hard goals: When you set hard goals, you set yourself up for failure, which translates into frustration and then potentially backsliding or totally giving up. There are too many variables that the value stream cannot control to make hard goals realistic. Instead focus on making sure your value stream metrics are trending in the right direction.

Value stream leaders need autonomy to be little general managers: If they have people or equipment assigned to their value stream that they do not ultimately control, then it will create undesirable conflict and frustration. The whole group needs to march to one drummer; the value stream leader. **Put as much of your costs as possible directly into the value streams:** Expect resistance, particularly in the office areas, to the concept of putting the value stream first. By definition, anyone not in a value stream is waste and something the customer does not want to pay for; consequently, strive for as little non-value stream support as possible.

Use the five principles of lean as your criteria to make decisions: "If you adhere to these principles, you will truly be pursuing perfection; the fifth principle of lean.

The Five Principles of Lean

1. **Identify Customers and Specify Value:** The starting point is to recognise that only a small fraction of the total time and effort in any organisation actually adds value for the end customer. By clearly defining Value for a specific product or service from the end customer's perspective, all the non value activities or waste can be targeted for removal.

2. **Identify and Map the Value Stream:** The Value Stream is the entire set of activities across all parts of the organisation involved in jointly delivering the product or service. This represents the end-to-end process that delivers the value to the customer. Once you understand what your customer wants the

147

next step is to identify how you are delivering (or not) that to them.

3. **Create Flow by Eliminating Waste:** Typically when you first map the Value Stream you will find that only 5% of activities add value, this can rise to 45% in a service environment. Eliminating this waste ensures that your product or service "flows" to the customer without any interruption, detour or waiting.

4. **Respond to Customer Pull:** This is about understanding the customer demand on your service and then creating your process to respond to this. Such that you produce only what the customer wants when the customer wants it.

5. **Pursue Perfection:** Creating flow and pull starts with radically reorganising individual process steps, but the gains become truly significant as all the steps link together. As this happens more and more layers of waste become visible and the process continues towards the theoretical end point of perfection, where every asset and every action adds value for the end customer.

In following these five principles of Lean you will implement a philosophy that will become "just the way things are done". You are ensuring that you are driving towards the overall organisational strategy by constant review of your processes to ensure that they are constantly and consistently delivering value to your customer. This allows the organisation to maintain its high level of service whilst being able to grow and flex with a changing environment and it does this through implementing sustainable change.

While most companies introduce lean accounting after having some success with lean manufacturing, there is a strong argument for introducing lean accounting at the very beginning of your company's lean journey.

If a company introduces thoroughly lean performance measurements and accounting, control and improvement methods built around lean thinking, and then their lean transformation in manufacturing and throughout the organization will be much smoother and more thorough.

Chapter 25: Conclusion

It makes sense for a manufacturing company employing lean principles to also employ lean accounting. That is because typical financial reporting and cost accounting doesn't really support lean manufacturing efforts. The idea behind lean accounting is to optimize lean performance by providing more relevant information for decision-making.

A Different Focus

Lean accounting is designed to concentrate on the measures that matter to lean organizations primarily focused on continuous improvement. The same principles that impact the shop floor are translated to the back office:

- **Customer value:** What is the customer willing to pay for?
- **Value streams:** What steps are required to deliver customer value?
- **Flow:** How can the value stream be organized to flow seamlessly from beginning to end?
- **Pull:** How can the value stream respond to an upstream customer?
- **Perfection:** How can the organization improve a little bit every day?

This "big picture" thinking does not focus on departments or departmental efficiency. Instead, it focuses on the organization itself and its value streams, which include everything that contributes to creating value for a customer.

Traditional vs. Lean

Lean accounting methods and costing strategies fit a lean organization better than traditional methods and strategies. For example, in traditional accounting, the focus is on standard costs at the product level. With that in mind, standard rates are set and rarely updated. Overhead is applied to individual products using a standard rate based on labour hours, and the organization carefully tracks production costs.

With lean accounting, labour and overhead are generally incurred in the same period that products are sold. The organization tracks incremental profits from new business generated through each value stream. Pricing decisions are made based on understanding the market and customer value, and product costing is based on product features and characteristics.

Lean accounting also promotes simple, easy-to-understand reporting, quicker response times and flexibility. For example, month-end closes using lean accounting may take three days versus ten to 20 days using traditional accounting methods. This speed is accomplished by focusing on accuracy rather than precision, and by making entries throughout the month rather than waiting until month-end. Hard closes, meanwhile, are done quarterly. This timeliness enables the organization to respond more quickly to trends or hiccups, and contributes to a culture of continuous improvement.

A Visual Scorecard Approach

Lean accounting reporting often takes a visual "scorecard" approach, providing decision-makers with the exact measures they need in terms of operations, capacity, financial results and customer engagement. While the accounting team still prepares traditional financial statements for lenders and others who need them, lean accounting strips out a lot of the fixed costs so that internal leaders can quickly see current numbers.

Is this type of accounting for you? It depends on your company's structure and interest in going "lean" in your manufacturing processes. If you are already a lean organization, lean accounting is likely a natural fit.

Financial Worries? Take Action with Lean NOW!

Many are currently quaking in their boots about the viability of their company during this confusing and complex global economic downturn.

All of us are worried about cash since it is the grease that makes our business engine run smoothly, and now more than ever, we need to maximize its availability and use it prudently.

Further, since applying lean thinking to processes often conserves cash, you probably should ask, "How can our lean efforts help us RIGHT NOW?" While lean at a macro level is a long term culture transformation, there are focused actions to consider when trying to free up cash.

Below are few suggestions on how to conserve cash or use it very wisely to maintain your business engine so it does not sputter or even seize up and stop!

Only Make What You Can Sell

Scrutinize every production order to ensure it is for items that are needed based on true customer demand. Ensure you are not producing items based on production orders created by the MRP system using potentially outdated forecasts.

Reduce your batch sizes to match the demand rate. Often batch sizes are set to reduce the number of set ups based on assumptions that the equipment needs to be kept running all the time, or based on maximum internal capacity. Unfortunately demand is usually lower than capacity, so you should decrease your batch sizes and increase your set ups so that you are not making excess units based on some outdated batch size calculation.

Talk to your customers to establish demand. Ensure that their needs and demands are not changing. They are in the same economy, so you do not want to take outdated forecasts and use them to consume your resources. Ensure there is good visibility to your customers real demand rate where ever and as often as possible.

Buy Only What You Need

Rethink your strategy of finding low cost materials or service suppliers. Look to local suppliers who can offer smaller units more frequently. New customers are also of great value to suppliers right now, so you might also get some very attractive pricing. Even if you pay more for smaller volumes delivered more frequently, it can significantly improve your cash flow.

Implement external kan-ban. This is the practice of re-ordering based on the actual consumption of materials rather than forecasted usage. Forecast usage ordering in nearly every case will increase your purchase of raw materials. Create "pull" (lean thinking) with your suppliers!

Root out Work In Process Excess

The first place inventory drops with lean thinking is when you link your production areas to create flow. If you have done this, then you have already realized this tremendous benefit. But if you are like many, you still have opportunity here. One quick way to ensure you do not have unintended WIP is to take three steps:

1. Ensure you never start production of an item unless you have all the materials in house to complete the item. Far too frequently, production stops because of lack of the right materials at the right place at the right time. When this happens, production stops; wasting all the efforts that have gone before.

155

2. Ensure your equipment is ready to go when you are. Start some Total Productive Maintenance activities. The second area of unintended WIP is when an item is started and then the equipment breaks down, is not ready to produce, or has no people assigned to the job. Again, when this happens, production stops. And, the cash stops flowing too.

3. Reduce batch size until you get your equipment near capacity. Any batch larger than one that does not make equipment or personnel over capacity is both an increase in material consumption and an increase in lead-time. Most traditional thinking does not understand this point. So, try it out now if your demand is low a "free lesson" in lean.

Collect the Money

A tried and true method to help the cash crunch is to collect the money owed to you for products and services already provided. The normal method is to call up the customers and beg them to pay. This is often a pathetic activity when you consider that the number one reason that customers do not pay is because there is a defect in the invoice that is sent to the customer. Over and over again, we find that when an improvement event (kaizen) is focused on the invoice to cash process, we identify significant waste and gaps in the process that keeps the cash in the customer hand, and not in yours. Launch a kaizen event now on this topic.

Measure the Right Stuff

Now more than ever, it is imperative to ensure you have the right measurements. If you use standard cost accounting you will not have the information you need to manage the business and cash flow of the company. Standard cost accounting thinking has no focus on the customer and thereby will cause you to over produce in nearly every circumstance.

In fact if you do the actions listed above, standard cost measures will actively tell the organization that they are the WRONG actions to do. Immediately switch your focus to what you ship and not what you produce. Look at your actual spending categories; wages, benefits, utilities, scrap, supplies, etc rather than your performance to standard cost measures. Remember, these measures are set to consume all your capacity, and not to control your cash.

Paying people to produce excess product costs more than paying people to produce nothing. Use any idle time to clean, train, implement improvements to process, improve workplace organization, and make progress on important initiatives that are behind schedule.

You and your organization cannot afford to overproduce.

Keep improving!!

Resource and References

Shigeo Shingo, Norman Bodek, Collin McLoughlin: Kaizen and the Art of Creative Thinking - The Scientific Thinking Mechanism

Shigeo Shingo; Fundamental Principles of Lean Manufacturing

Shigeo Shingo, Andrew P. Dillon (Translator); Zero Quality Control: Source Inspection and the Poka-yoke System

Shigeo Shingo; Non-Stock Production: The Shingo System of Continuous Improvement

Shigeo Shingo; A Study of the Toyota Production System from an Industrial Engineering Viewpoint

Shigeo Shingo; A Study of the Toyota Production System from an Industrial Engineering Viewpoint

Lessons from Toyota's long drive, an interview with Katsuaki Watanabe, HBR, July 2007

Liker, J. & D. Meier, Toyota Talent, McGraw Hill, 2007

Shook, J. , Managing To Learn, Lean Enterprise Institute 2008

Fishman, C., "No Satisfaction", Fast Company, Dec 2006/Jan 2007